*How to Make
Up to $100 an Hour
Every Hour You Work*

How to Make Up to $100 an Hour Every Hour You Work

John Stockwell

Parker Publishing Company, Inc.

West Nyack, New York

© 1979 *by*

PARKER PUBLISHING COMPANY, INC.

West Nyack, New York

All rights reserved. No part of this book may be reproduced in any form or by any means, without permission in writing from the publisher.

Library of Congress Cataloging in Publication Data

Stockwell, John.
  How to make up to $100 an hour every hour you work.

  Includes index.
  1. Success. 2. Self-employed. 3. Small business.
I. Title.
HF5386.S882   650'.12   79-14910
ISBN 0-13-423533-9

Printed in the United States of America

Other Books by the Author:

100 Ways to Make Money in Your Spare Time, Starting with Less than $100

How to Borrow Everything You need to Build a Great Personal Fortune

How to Double and Triple the Useful Life of Everything You Own

how this book may help you make up to $100 an hour . . . every hour you work

How often have you dreamed of having an extra $100 to splurge on some luxury? How often have you thought what life would be like if you could double your present salary or earnings? Almost everyone has dreams such as these. Now I am going to ask you to imagine something big: suppose you could earn up to *$100 an hour . . . every hour you worked*. How would your life change?

Your present dream of an extra week's vacation could turn into months of luxurious travel to far-off places. . . .

Your thoughts of a small second car could become a decision between Cadillacs or Lincolns. . . .

Your wish to fly to some vacation spot might become more spectacular when you land in your own plane. . . .

Dreams such as these are possible

These are not idle dreams. Most certainly not. I am going to tell you how other people have achieved such dreams—people whose talents, education, and family advantages are probably not much different from yours. With their success stories, I will reveal to you their methods, techniques, and other shortcuts that propelled them to wealth. And, I will show you *every step to take to duplicate their successes*. For example:

Warren B. is a person you will meet in these pages. As a clerk in the personnel department of a large company, Warren wasn't starving, but he was hard put to buy much beyond the necessities of daily life. Then Warren discovered one of the shortcuts I describe in this book, and soon his life became one of plenty and contentment.

Warren didn't even stop working immediately; he simply couldn't believe he could make so much money on his own—and with so little work. His work on his own venture took a few hours a week, usually no more than ten hours.

While Warren didn't hit the $100-an-hour target at once, he did figure his time as being close to $80 an hour, every hour he worked. At that rate, his annual income, apart from his regular job was pushing $40,000 a year. This was more than three times what he was earning at the plant—with only one-fourth the working time. And he was his own boss! Needless to say, Warren eventually left the plant to devote full time to this and other ventures.

How the Power Shortcuts to wealth can help you

Warren B. discovered and used a "Power Shortcut." When he stumbled on it he knew it would work ... not only for him, but for others as well. This book is built around such shortcuts and how they worked for people like Warren.

The Power Shortcuts have been called the "methods of the millionaires." This doesn't mean you have to have money to exploit them to the fullest. Rather, they are methods that can be used by most anyone with modest capital to amass a great personal fortune.

Some of the shortcuts are ways of borrowing money, so you can really start from "ground zero" in your quest for wealth. Many of these shortcuts are true "insider's secrets" because no one has wanted to reveal them as I am going to in the pages that follow.

These Power Shortcuts can be used by anyone—

- persons with little or no capital
- people with little formal training or business experience
- individuals who missed many of the opportunities of life

The Power Shortcuts can build an "automatic income" for life

The stories you read in the pages that follow will tell you of people who have built great wealth in businesses and enterprises of their own. But, do not look for business "plans" in this book. Instead, you will get the *Power Shortcuts most likely to make you rich.*

Here are just a few of the success stories that can inspire and help you—

- Using the Power Shortcut described in Chapter 3, Ken L. went from a $6-an-hour plumber's helper to an expert in a needed service in his community. He's the "professional" people call when they have problems, and he has seen his income climb to over $100 an hour.
- Carry W. used to do drudge typing for around $4 an hour. With the information revealed in Chapter 4, she now provides a much wider business service to important people in her university town. In doing this, she increased her income ten times—to $40 an hour.
- Ray R. hated the thought of painting his own house, and the alternative of paying high prices for a professional painter to do the job. In Chapter 4 you will see the Power Shortcut Ray used to put himself in the housepainting business—a business that earns him $77.50 an hour and he never touches a brush!
- A basement workshop and an interest in building birdhouses was the source of independence and wealth for Fred G. whom you will meet in Chapter 8. Among other things, his business generates a mailing list that he rents to non-competitors. Income from this activity runs to thousands of dollars a year,

but he does *zero work* for this money—it's all handled by a broker who sends him frequent big-money checks.
- Tom H. built a sparetime business that eventually was earning him about $180 a week. People said he was crazy when he applied the Power Shortcut described in Chapter 6 because his income temporarily dropped down to $40 a week. But, this same Power Shortcut actually enabled him to quickly build his sparetime income up to $240 a week. Best of all, all he had to do was to collect the money; other people were actually doing the work!

Power Shortcuts can help you earn up to $100 an hour

These are but a few of the personal stories which show how the Power Shortcuts worked for others, and how they can work for you. They demonstrate exactly why I believe and say that it is entirely possible for a person to earn up to $100 for every hour he or she spends using these Power Shortcuts.

Build an "automatic income" for life without risk

You've probably heard of people who risked everything in starting some new venture—people who quit their jobs . . . mortgaged themselves to the hilt . . . and skated on a thin line between failure and success for a long time. Is this what you have to do to make it big? Absolutely not! The

Power Shortcuts can be used without risk to your present status, job, or financial security.

Like Warren B., who worked in the company personnel department, you can keep your present job until you're sure you want to make a move. That move can be out of a hum-drum job . . . out of a cramped apartment to a larger home . . . or even out to another part of the country.

You can start today . . . this very minute . . . building your dreams of success without doing anything more than spending the few hours necessary to read this book from cover to cover. This book will show you how these Power Shortcuts can virtually produce an *automatic income for life for you.*

Personal action techniques insure your success

However, just reading this book will not make you rich. Even I can't promise you that. You must supply one simple ingredient—*personal action.*

This book will be your guide, but you must supply the "doing." What I can promise you is this—the Power Shortcuts will enable you to achieve your dreams of success with far less effort than you may think is necessary. Very quickly you will discover that you can start applying these techniques without sacrificing your job, your family, or your everyday pleasures.

But, remember this—there is one shortcut you must avoid. Don't skip hastily through this book. Read it from beginning to end, and in detail. You must be aware of what each of the Power Shortcuts can do for you, and how you can put more than one to work for you at a single time. Once you have read this book thoroughly, you can seek out opportunities, and with your inside know-how, turn them to your financial advantage.

The few hours you spend with this book might easily be worth far more than $100 an hour. Indeed, your investment of reading time might eventually be worth $1000 . . . $10,000 . . . perhaps even $100,000 an hour for every hour you spent within these pages.

Good luck!

John Stockwell

contents

how this book may help you make up to $100 an hour . . . every hour you work • 7

Dreams such as these are possible • How the Power Shortcuts to wealth can help you • The Power shortcuts can build an "automatic income" for life • Power Shortcuts can help you earn up to $100 an hour • Build an "automatic income" for life without risk • Personal action techniques insure your success

1 the easy-to-learn secret of zooming your income to $100 an hour • 19

$100 an hour is no idle dream • How much money do you earn every hour you work? • Master rate charts • You can have anything you want from life • How you can reach the goals you choose • What must you do to make $100 an hour? • It's never too late to become rich • Your personal wealth plan • How much is your time worth? • Using the skills you already have to earn up to $100 an hour • How one man made it big • Why it is often easier to make $100 an hour than $10 an hour • Are you too busy working to become truly rich? • How to "think" your way to a million • A simple trick for getting new ideas • Understanding the Magic Money Pyramid • Making a year's pay in a few months • Earn the top rate because you are the boss • How to discover all you need to know to make $100 an hour

2 **finding the good-luck magnet that is sure to attract success for you • 45**

What this will mean to you • Keeping risks at a minimum • How to find the right wealth path for you • How to use luck to gain a $100-an-hour income • What is a Power Shortcut? • A Power Shortcut gives you the leverage you need to build wealth • How to use power shortcuts in every business venture • Make success a habit • Using the Power Shortcuts to cut 20% to 80% from the time needed for financial success • How to get the most for your time • Measuring the value of your time • Finding the best place to work • Using the Power Shortcuts without doing any of the actual work yourself • How to use the Power Shortcuts to get all the money you need • How to make people want to work for your success

3 **easy ways to smash the barriers keeping you from a big income • 65**

Smashing the barriers to wealth • How to remove the one obstacle to your $100-an-hour income • Attacking the problems that keep you from success • Discovering the hidden wealth-building power within you • How to achieve the image of success • Getting your picture in the paper • How you can make it big by joining the experts • How to make success a habit

4 **the 3-step formula that virtually guarantees you a $100-an-hour income • 82**

How to use the Three-Step Formula to attain your goals • Maximize your profit potential • Personal involvement means fast profits • Turning the Power Shortcuts into long-term investments • Maximize your hourly income by specializing • How to Pyramid Power Shortcuts for fast, personal profit • How to get free professional advice for the business you choose • Hitting the $100-an-hour target

contents

5 how to use OPM to shorten your climb to $100-an-hour income • 97

How to make Other People's Money work for you • How to make lenders want to give you all the money you need • How to have instant cash when you need it • 21 Common and not so common money sources you can tap • How to get more money when you are already in debt

6 using people leverage to help you earn up to $100 an hour • 113

Using the master Power Shortcut to reach your $100-an-hour goal • Putting the secret of the master Power Shortcut to work • Smashing the barriers to a $100-an-hour income • Using many people to help you grow • How P/L Techniques free you for big, important jobs • Harnessing the multiplier effect of P/L Techniques • P/L Techniques can assure quick success

7 how to earn up to $100 an hour working from your home • 128

Get SMART—make a fortune in a home business • How a business phone and some stationery can put you in a profitable home business • How to discover opportunities that need no space • Discovering opportunities that need no investment • Finding the right home-based business for you • 100 ways to make money in your spare time starting with less than $100

8 how to make up to $100 an hour in mail order • 144

How to avoid the most common pitfall in mail order • How one person started a successful mail-order business with only a $20 bill • The 100-postcard trick for discovering hot mail-order ideas • Deciding on a product or services to sell • A fortune from Specialized Newsletters • Developing a sure-fire formula for a successful offer • Two steps to mail-order success • Mail-order millions in magazines and mailing lists • Finding the right publication in which to advertise • A mail-order pro's secret of

8   how to make up to $100 an hour in mail order (cont.)

picking a successful mailing list • the "1 to 10 scale" of rating mailing lists • BEST—Scale of 10 • VERY GOOD—Scale of 6 to 7 • FAIR to POOR—Scale of 4 to 5 • VERY POOR—Scale of 1 to 3 • How to discover "hot" mailing lists with 3 simple testing techniques • Taking the big step up to $100-an-hour income in mail order • Building repeat income in mail order • Getting more income from each customer

9   tested "success secret" techniques that can make $100 an hour possible for you • 173

Direct mail cost checklist • Printing • Circular handling • Postage • List rental • Add costs carefully • How much should you expect? • How to make a test mailing pay off • How many lists should you test? • How many names should you test on a list? • Important first impressions • Color • Message • How to write copy that sells • How to use this four-part formula to sell more • Hey! • You! • See? • So! • Others secrets of mail-order success • mail order success on a shoestring • Making deals with a printer • Making deals with magazines for free advertising

10   how to earn up to $100 an hour while working for someone else • 195

How to work your way up to $100 an hour • How to find time to make $100 an hour while working for someone else • Wasted hours can be wealth hours • Checklist of wealth hours available to you • Set up a plan for regular work • How to discover profitable ideas while working for someone else • Getting rich by asking questions • Simple ideas on the job can bring you a fortune

11   using the power shortcuts to build an automatic income for life • 210

The Power Shortcuts • Timing • Building up to $100 an hour

index • 215

*How to Make
Up to $100 an Hour
Every Hour You Work*

1

the easy-to-learn secret of zooming your income to $100 an hour

When was the last time you saw an ad in a newspaper offering a job paying $100 an hour?

We're willing to bet that you have never seen such an ad. After all, $100 an hour for a 40 hour week amounts to $288,000 a year. That's more than the President of the United States earns in salary.

But, how many millionaires are there in the country today, and how many of these people made it themselves, without the help of anyone else? It has been estimated that several thousand people become millionaires each year, and of course many thousands more make close to this figure. But, these people don't make big money by answering an ad and working for someone else.

Who, then, is making this big money, and how are they making it? It could be one of your neighborhood friends. Don't scoff! That quiet guy down the street, living an apparently simple life in his two-bedroom house might just be making $100 an hour.

Don't be fooled by the outward appearances of those who must tell you all the time that they are rich. They might be making good money, but the chances are that they are nowhere near earning $100 an hour—your goal, and hopefully your reward for reading this book.

$100 an hour is no idle dream

How often have you heard someone say this: "There are doers and talkers in this world, and it's the doers who make out." So many little phrases are drummed into each of us as we go through life, that we never really think about their true meaning. But, this phrase should be remembered as you read each page of this book. We are going to give you what has been called the "methods of the millionaires," but unless you do something about using them, you will never get much more than your weekly paycheck.

However, because you are reading this book, you have shown that you do have the drive to succeed—the drive to make $100 an hour. We are going to tell you the stories of many people who have, by their own efforts, and by using the techniques we will reveal in these pages, made their dream of $100 an hour come true. And, as you read each story, you will learn about a different Power Shortcut to wealth. In Chapter 2, we will describe the idea behind the Power Shortcuts; we will tell you what they are, how to use them, and how to develop Power Shortcuts that you can use every day of your wealth-building life.

But, before we get into the details of the Power Shortcuts and the stories of those who have developed and used them to make millions of dollars, we want you to read every page of this chapter very carefully. The simple, tested background on which you will build and use your Power Shortcuts must be clearly understood—as soon as possible.

the easy-to-learn secret of zooming your income to $100 an hour   21

How much money do you earn every hour you work?

Before you do anything, you should know what you *now* make every hour you work. This is important because it will show you how to set goals for attaining your dream of $100 an hour. If you are already paid by the hour, then you know what this figure is.

However, many persons are paid by the week or the month, and it is surprising how many such people have no idea what they make each hour they work. Below are Master Rate Charts especially computed for readers of this book. To use these charts first answer these two questions:

1) Do you work 35 hours or 40 hours a week?
2) Regardless of how or when you receive your paycheck, is your wage or salary figured on a weekly or monthly basis?

Depending on your answers to these two questions, choose the correct chart to find out your hourly rate.

Master rate charts

- If your rate is *weekly* and you work *35 hours* a week, use Table A
- If your rate is *weekly* and you work *40 hours* a week, use Table B
- If your rate is *monthly* and you work *35 hours* a week, use Table C
- If your rate is *monthly* and you work *40 hours* a week, use Table D

TABLE A (35-Hour Work Week)

If your weekly rate is:	This is what you earn each hour:
$100	$ 2.86
$125	$ 3.57
$150	$ 4.29
$175	$ 5.00
$200	$ 5.71
$225	$ 6.43
$250	$ 7.14
$275	$ 7.86
$300	$ 8.57
$325	$ 9.29
$350	$10.00
$375	$10.71
$400	$11.43
$425	$12.14
$450	$12.86
$475	$13.57
$500	$14.29

TABLE B (40-Hour Work Week)

If your weekly rate is:	This is what you earn each hour:
$100	$ 2.50
$125	$ 3.13
$150	$ 3.75
$175	$ 4.38
$200	$ 5.00

TABLE B (40-Hour Work Week) (*continued*)

If your weekly rate is:	This is what you earn each hour:
$225	$ 5.63
$250	$ 6.25
$275	$ 6.88
$300	$ 7.50
$325	$ 8.13
$350	$ 8.75
$375	$ 9.38
$400	$10.00
$425	$10.63
$450	$11.25
$475	$11.88
$500	$12.50

TABLE C (35-Hour Work Week)

If your monthly rate is:	This is what you earn each hour:
$400	$ 2.64
$425	$ 2.80
$450	$ 2.97
$475	$ 3.13
$500	$ 3.30
$550	$ 3.63
$600	$ 3.96
$650	$ 4.29
$700	$ 4.62
$750	$ 4.95

TABLE C (35-Hour Work Week) (*continued*)

If your monthly rate is:	This is what you earn each hour:
$800	$ 5.27
$850	$ 5.60
$900	$ 5.93
$950	$ 6.26
$1000	$ 6.59
$1100	$ 7.25
$1200	$ 7.91
$1300	$ 8.57
$1400	$ 9.23
$1500	$ 9.89
$1600	$10.55
$1700	$11.21
$1800	$11.87
$1900	$12.53
$2000	$13.19

TABLE D (40-Hour Work Week)

If your monthly rate is:	This is what you earn each hour:
$400	$ 2.31
$425	$ 2.45
$450	$ 2.60
$475	$ 2.74
$500	$ 2.88
$550	$ 3.17
$600	$ 3.46
$650	$ 3.75

TABLE D (40-Hour Work Week) *(continued)*

If your monthly rate is:	This is what you earn each hour:
$700	$ 4.04
$750	$ 4.33
$800	$ 4.62
$850	$ 4.90
$900	$ 5.19
$950	$ 5.48
$1000	$ 5.77
$1100	$ 6.35
$1200	$ 6.92
$1300	$ 7.50
$1400	$ 8.08
$1500	$ 8.65
$1600	$ 9.23
$1700	$ 9.81
$1800	$10.38
$1900	$10.96
$2000	$11.54

You can have anything you want from life

Some people are quite content with an ordinary existence; others want the best that life has to offer. Most people fall somewhere in the middle. Most of these people feel it takes special talents or luck to become rich, so they just drift. And, this is what keeps even the best intentions from turning into wealth.

Money means different things to different people, but

with $100 an hour, you can decide what it means to you and what you will do with it. However, simply saying that you want to earn the $100 an hour is only part of the job. You must set up some very specific goals for yourself. Setting a goal of earning $100 an hour is only the first step. Unless you have a clear picture of what this money will mean to you and what you intend to do with it, your chances of making it are slim.

How you can reach the goals you choose

Whatever you decide to do to make the $100 an hour, your main goal must always be that of making big money. Without this goal we can truthfully say that you will never get near your goal. Here are just a few of the important things that goals will do for you:

- Goals serve as your personal wealth map, pointing the direction for your money-making activity.
- Goals show you when you are going off course and help you get back on the track.
- Goals help you keep tabs on your progress.
- Goals remind you of the rewards you will get.

Some people find it easy to set goals, and do it almost automatically. But, even these people often find it helpful to write out their wealth objectives. As a starter, we'd like you to sit down right now, get a piece of paper, and write out your goals on it. We'll give you a little help in the form of this checklist, which you should copy on your paper:

1. I would like to make $____ per hour.
2. I would like to be making this money by ___(date)___.
3. I am willing to devote ___(hours)___ a day to this goal.
4. I will finish reading this book by ___(date)___.

Do yourself a favor right now. Write this goal checklist with your own personal information on a separate piece of paper and tuck it in the back of this book. Don't leave it there though. We want you to take it out and read it each time before you start a chapter in this book. By referring to this paper, you will constantly be reminded of your goals as the various Power Shortcuts are revealed to you. And, you will do your best to accomplish the important goal of reading and understanding the tested wealth-producing ideas in this book.

What must you do to make $100 an hour?

Make no mistake about it, you will have to work at building your $100 an hour income, but it will be fun all the way. The chances are that you will have to give up something at least temporarily. Your bowling night, perhaps, or a vacation, or the time you have been spending with a hobby. But, you will see as you get into your wealth-building activities, that they will be more fun than any hobby, and that you will kick yourself for not having started sooner.

It's never too late to become rich

Let's dispel the problem of age immediately. Some people make millions before their twentieth birthday and others after their eightieth. Oilman J. Paul Getty was worth several millions by his mid-twenties, and Col. Saunders built his Kentucky Fried Chicken business into a multi-million dollar success after he started collecting Social Security. Age is not a barrier; health is not a barrier and previous success is the least important indicator of future success when you harness the strength of the Power Shortcuts.

The important thing to keep in mind is that you have decided that you *do* want to earn up to $100 an hour, and now you must clearly decide what it will cost you to achieve this goal. The chances are that you are now working, but are simply not satisfied with your progress and prospects. You might be working at an ordinary job, or you may even be a lawyer or other highly-paid professional. Whatever your situation, the work of building wealth will be the same. And, as we have said, it makes no difference what you are now doing, or what your educational or achievement level has been, you can, by using the Power Shortcuts in this book make your goal of $100 an hour come true.

Your personal wealth plan

Think, for a moment, what it would be like to temporarily give up your hobby, or bowling night, or a loafing Saturday. It might seem bleak because of the relief such change offers from your present job. But now think of what you might be able to do, instead of this dreary work, if you had an income of $100 an hour. At this point, most people who seriously consider making $100 an hour, begin to make up a list of the things they will have to give up in order to devote the time to building a $100 an hour income. And, they also make a second list which details all of the things that they would be able to do with this money that they cannot do now on their present income.

It doesn't take much imagination to see that any such list automatically becomes a "Wealth Plan." We suggest that you begin right now to write your own Personal Wealth Plan.

How much is your time worth?

A short while back we showed you how to figure your current on-the-job hourly rate of pay. If you're like most folks your first reaction was probably one of despair—$100 an hour seems pretty steep compared to what you're actually earning now.

Take heart! The first thing to realize is that you don't charge the same rate for work you do in your own business as what your boss pays you. Your boss pays you and still has plenty left over for profit for himself *from your work*. When you work for yourself, you should pocket *all* this money. Even in a beginning venture this can mean much.

For example: Ken L. was a plumber's helper who came to our home to unstop a clogged drain. Counting travel time from the shop the job took about an hour. The bill from his boss came to $45! Now you know that Ken earns nowhere near $45 an hour. If he's lucky, his boss is paying him $6 to $7 an hour. This means his boss is earning $37 to $39 every hour Ken works for him.

His boss also has enough work to keep three helpers pretty busy. Three times $37 means $111 an hour for a boss who doesn't get dirty, drives a new Continental, and takes winter vacations in Switzerland!

While watching Ken clean the drain, we mentioned this fact to him. Ken is bright and hard working, but the thought that he could do the work himself as his own boss and pocket all the money, never occurred to him. You can bet it didn't take Ken long to start up his own business, and before much time had passed, he, too, had helpers working for him, helping him climb to $100 an hour. More about him later.

Now, of course, you're saying you're not interested in going into the dirty business of cleaning stopped drains. We're not suggesting you should. We gave you Ken's story because it illustrates several important points that you should keep in mind as we suggest business opportunities:

1) You will never get rich working for someone else. Right now you have to realize there is no job, short of being a surgeon or a top-flight Wall Street lawyer, that will pay you anywhere near $100 an hour.

2) People are accustomed to paying for most services much more than the actual workman could possibly make in an hour of work. Cleaning a drain was worth $45 to us, especially since a flood of dirty water could have ruined thousands of dollars of valuable house furnishings. A ten-minute job fixing a loose wire in a car was worth $15 because of the inconvenience it prevented on a vacation. You can recall similar examples in your own experience.

3) In the beginning, you will probably have to do all the work yourself in any business you pick. At the very least, start by charging at least *twice*, or even *three times*, what you normally earn in your regular job. Use the Master Rate Charts as a guide. As you progress and add helpers, you can increase that figure, and your customers will readily accept your prices as we showed in the examples above.

4) As you add helpers or employees, you pyramid your earnings in rapid fashion. Let's say you are running a carpet-cleaning business. You charge $25 to clean a 9-by-12 rug—a job which takes perhaps an hour. Materials and supplies cost a dollar, so you earn $24 cleaning that rug. If you work at this job yourself, you'll always earn $24 an hour as a top income figure. But, if you prosper and add five helpers, paying them each $6 an hour, you're clearing about $18 an hour for each man who works for you. Five times $18 an hour comes to $90 an hour—a lot closer to $100 an hour than you may have thought possible.

This last point is the secret of making a big hourly income. Test the opportunity you think you would like the best. See if you can make it work for yourself. Then, assuming it does work, pyramid your hourly earnings up, up, and UP by *adding more people doing the same job.*

It takes a lot of effort to make big money, but once you get used to the idea of making $100 an hour, the work becomes easy, and most who have done it, find themselves working harder than they ever worked—but enjoying it more than anything else they ever did. You see, they are now doing something they like—something which not only earns them $100 an hour, but rewards them richly for their effort.

Using the skills you already have to earn up to $100 an hour

Most people think that those who earn up to $100 an hour are doctors, lawyers, and other highly-paid professionals—but this simply isn't true. It is possible for just about anyone who has the ambition to earn this big money. In fact, there are many professionals who never made this kind of money until they turned to the techniques we describe in this book and are now wealthy.

As we have already said, it is all but impossible to make $100 an hour with a paycheck from an employer. So, this means that you will have to do something other than what you are now doing to make this money. But, remember, it may not be necessary to leave your job to do this. You may want to test your wealth-building skills with the Power Shortcuts as you continue in your present job, or you may even want to stay in your work and use these powerful techniques in your spare time simply to make extra money.

There are many people who have decided to stay with the company that has employed them for years in order to take advantage of a pension plan, but have used our methods to greatly supplement their salary—and pension—after retirement.

How one man made it big

Carl L. had worked for a huge chemical company for most of his life. He made about $8 an hour, but found that he could never acquire the things that make life infinitely more comfortable—a summer home, second car, boat, and a high-priced camera he had wanted for many years. Carl's life was secure, but it lacked the comforts he and his wife often dreamed of. He even had a company-paid pension which he would receive when he retired, so the thought of striking out on his own after a fortune seemed kind of risky.

But Carl decided that he wanted the few things that would make his life more pleasurable, and he turned to a Power Shortcut described later in this book which helped him market products he was able to make at home and resell at a large profit. We would like to tell you Carl's full story right now, but in order to benefit from it fully, it is important that you first read and understand the next chapter which tells you what the Power Shortcuts are and how you can harness them to build great personal wealth.

But, we can tell you that Carl was not only able to supplement his income, but that he was able to build a spare-time fortune while keeping his job, and holding onto his job until his pension rights were fully vested.

We will bet you already have the skills needed to make $100 an hour. This may surprise you. It surprises most people, but they simply don't realize that it is not so much the work-a-day skill that makes a fortune, but rather the understanding and use of techniques of fortune making that leads one to wealth. This doesn't mean that you have to attend a large university and earn a degree in business. In fact, most people who study business in college seldom go on to make real big money. What we do mean is this; you must discover how to turn your present interests, abilities, and skills into money-making activities by using the Power Shortcuts. Each

the easy-to-learn secret of zooming your income to $100 an hour 33

Power Shortcut is, in itself, a mini-method of success. Each is a short route to a fortune—a method you can put to work without risking your present job.

Why it is often easier to make $100 an hour than $10 an hour

To some of our readers, even $10 an hour may seem like a worthwhile goal. But take it from those who have made really big money in a hurry—set your sights on a big income—don't settle for less.

The $10-an hour jobs exist—that's only $20,800 a year—and you can see them advertised every day in the newspaper. They usually demand quite a bit of training and experience. But, you should not want to settle for this—you can't build a true fortune on a paycheck. Therefore, while it may be tempting and appear somewhat easier to attain, don't settle for less than your goal—*$100 an hour.*

Now, we are beginning to get at the nub of the matter—$100 an hour. Suppose that you could work *half* the time and make the *same* money you are now being paid. You would, in effect, be earning *twice* your hourly rate. And, it would give you time to do other things as well.

The secret of making up to $100 an hour lies in using the Power Shortcuts which will be described in the next chapter and used in detail throughout the book.

In addition to the Power Shortcuts, we will show you how to make every minute make money for you. After all, if you are making $100 an your, it makes little sense to work a 40-hour week for the rest of your life. Therefore, the other important aspect of this book is to show you how to develop money-making opportunities that will let you make up to $100 an hour and only work for as many hours as you like.

Remember, when we say $100 an hour, we also mean:

1) Nearly two dollars a minute, $1.67 to be exact.

2) For an eight-hour day, it also equals $800.
3) If you work 35 hours a week, $100 an hour means $3500!

Some people have the drive to work hard at making $100 an hour, and they keep at it eight, ten, or more hours a day. Needless to say, these driving people quickly amass fortunes. We leave it up to you if you want to drive this hard. Our own feeling is that too much work leaves you with too little time to enjoy the fruits of your labors.

Each of the Power Shortcuts we describe has the potential for $100 an hour, and each will allow you to use as much or as little time as you see fit. However, the important point to remember is that when you turn on the power of a shortcut, you are not playing for nickels and dimes—you have the potential for really big money.

When you get used to the idea that it will be easier to make $100 an hour than $10 an hour, you will be on your way to reaching your goal.

Are you too busy working to become truly rich?

A wise man once commented that most people are too busy making a living to make a fortune.

Think about this for a moment!

You are working at your daily job; it keeps you busy and perhaps tired at the end of the day. But, when you read the stories we will tell you in the pages of this book, you will see that most of the people who have hit the $100-an-hour mark did it while working at another job for someone else. But, they did set goals, then did set aside time to get them moving, and they did stick to their idea of making $100 an hour.

Before you begin to put the power of the shortcuts to work for you, you will have to get rid of the ordinary ideas you now have about working. Not that you will be working any less, but that the routine of ordinary work is entirely different from the dynamics of using the Power Shortcuts to build incredible wealth. It may be hard to break this habit of thinking, particularly, if you are starting your wealth-building program on a part-time basis. But, it is the thinking that is important. *You must think wealth*—not the thoughts you are used to thinking in your present job, but the thoughts which free you to put the Power Shortcuts to work for you immediately.

How to "think" your way to a million

As we mentioned before, very few people actually plan their life goals, let alone pursue them. Rather, their thoughts are on short range achievements—a new car, boat, or a trip to a distant land. Furthermore, very few people actually think about themselves, except to come up with excuses for failure, or even marginal successes. But, in order to make a fortune, you must be comfortable with yourself, and everybody else.

Everyone wants to feel good about himself. And, it is possible for everybody to feel good about himself, without self deception, when he knows how to really look at himself.

Feeling good about oneself is an easy matter, even if everything seems to have gone wrong. In truth, feeling good about yourself is simply a matter of mentally listing all of your abilities and capabilities. You don't have to be world famous to feel that you have made significant achievements. Even though you may be feeling low about your accomplishments and prospects, we can guarantee you that there is enough in every person's life to give you that all-important feeling that you can make your goal of $100 an hour.

Here, in simple check-list form, are the most successful methods for putting yourself in the millionaire's frame of mind.

- Accept the the responsibility for everything you do. When something doesn't turn out the way you plan it, don't get bogged—try to figure out what went wrong. Was it your fault? Be honest! And, most important—what can you do to make it come out right the next time?
- Do you spend enough time with your projects? Merely having a good idea is not enough, unless you have an idea a minute and can sell them to someone else. What this boils down to is motivation. When you set out to do something, make sure that you follow through, to the absolute best of your ability.
- Have an open mind. When you are working your way toward a $100 an hour income, you must keep your eyes and ears open. But, your eyes and ears are connected with your brain, and if you don't consider everything openly, you will miss many opportunities. Simply because someone else told you that such-and-such an idea would not work doesn't mean that it won't work for you.
- Often, the people who scoff at your thoughts are simply making excuses for not taking the steps themselves. Everyone laughed at the idea of the automobile, but just look at how many people are making a lot of money in one phase or another of this huge industry.
- Recognize and accept your own thoughts. Simply because you don't have a college education, have never made a fortune or are not as successful as you think you should be doesn't mean that the road to wealth is forever closed to you.
- So many people today are taught right from childhood that their ideas mean little—and that they must follow

the directions of others. These are the people who will be drawing a meager paycheck all of their lives—if they are lucky! Listen to your inner voice—but listen with a careful ear.
- Don't be impulsive; when you get an idea, run it over your mind and even talk it over with others. More often than not, a good idea will be stepped on by other people because they are jealous that they didn't think of it themselves—or that you just might make a fortune of it. What this all boils down to is this—train yourself to be a critical, but independent thinker.
- Think of yourself as a person who can do anything he wants. If you set reasonable goals—and $100 an hour is a reasonable goal for just about anyone—you can attain them. Don't dwell on past failures. And don't sit back and gloat over past successes. The $100 an hour goal can only be attained when you set your sights on it, use the Power Shortcuts, and push ahead, regardless of past problems, and the comments of those around you who are sure to be jealous.

A simple trick for getting new ideas

Later, when you are in the big money league, you can take trips to exotic foreign lands, but right now, we want you to take a number of short trips—and they won't cost you a cent. You are already taking one trip—through the pages of this book. As you read, new ideas will unfold to you, and you will see from the case histories how others with fewer advantages than you have had have made the journey to their goal of $100 an hour.

But, now for the mini-trips. If you are like most of the millions of other people in this country, your life has narrowed down to some pretty consistent habits. Up at 6. Breakfast. Then to work by 8:30. Lunch. Off at 4:30. Fight your way home through the traffic. Supper. An evening of TV, movies, or some hobby and then to bed. With only a few minor changes, this is a pretty accurate picture of the lives of many of us.

While most don't complain, many folks are aware that something is missing from their lives. And what is missing is different experiences. Try this simple test. If you drive a car to and from work, the chances are that you go the same route each day. You probably know every telephone pole and building on your route. It's comfortable and easy to do.

But now, we want you to pick another very different route—even if it is considerably out of your way. Drive slowly—observe—think, and when you get home try to remember what new things you saw. Nothing startling perhaps, but this simple exercise will open your mind to new ideas.

We told Harvey L., a friend, to do this, and on his first trip via a new route he told us that he spotted a dry-cleaning store that appeared to be pretty run-down. A few more trips by this store revealed that it was, indeed, on its last legs. Our friend had always thought about running a retail operation, so one day he worked up his courage and went into the store and offered to buy it.

To Harvey's surprise, the owner had thought of selling, but like most other people, had simply not done anything about it. He had simply lost interest in the business, and was at the point where the store would have folded in a few months anyway.

Harvey didn't have much money to invest, but the owner wasn't in a position to ask much either. As is common in many types of businesses, the physical part of the business—fixtures, signs, and what have you—were the bulk of the assets, and in this case did not amount to much. The actual cleaning was done by a large service company which provided pickups, deliveries, and cleaning on a wholesale basis.

The owner of the store accepted $2000 as a down payment, with $13,000 to be paid off from store receipts over a period of three years. At this point, although Harvey didn't know it, he intuitively employed a Power Shortcut we will discuss in detail later. Rather than quitting his job and trying to live on a modest income from a dry-cleaning store, Harvey hired part-timers—housewives and retired people who covered the store for a total of twelve hours a day, six days a week. They were glad to work for modest wages, and after paying all expenses, Harvey was clearing perhaps a dollar an hour each hour the store was open.

Understanding the Magic Money Pyramid

Your first comment might be, "A dollar an hour is crazy!" But look at it this way: Harvey was working only a few hours a week for this money which came to $72 a week. At an hour or so a day, Harvey was working six hours a week and earning $72. That's $12 an hour—or over $475 a week if you translate it into a regular, 40-hour-a-week job. Right off, this was more than Harvey was earning in his regular job on an hourly basis.

For the time he spent, Harvey was very well paid. But he didn't stop there. Having discovered the secret of people making money for you, he quickly developed what we call the Magic Money Pyramid: *Whenever you find a successful way to make money, see how you can double, triple, or multiply the operation many times over to increase your income.*

What Harvey did was simple. He looked for more dry-cleaning stores in other parts of town and later in adjoining towns. With a record of success in one store, he was able to borrow money for additional outlets, each time pyramiding his income upwards. After a time, it was clear to Harvey he would have to devote full time to his chain of dry-cleaning stores. A dozen stores, last time we heard, were grossing something like one-and-a-half-million dollars a year. He has become a wholesale cleaner himself serving other stores, and you can bet his income is well over $100 an hour now.

Unlike Harvey, who rode to work everyday, you might want to take a business seeking trip right in your living room. Most newspapers have a Business Opportunities column in which owners advertise businesses they wish to sell. Read and answer some of the ads, even if the price is way over your head. You would probably be surprised at what can work out for you.

Making a year's pay in a few months

A time-clock job will never make you a fortune; but, by altering your outlook, as we have described, it may be possible for you to make a year's pay in a few months.

Look at the case of Jerry K. Jerry was stationed at a Navy base in a very pleasant resort area. When he received his discharge, he decided to settle in the area. He had been a cook in the Navy, and naturally turned to cooking in civilian life. Because the Navy doesn't train their cooks to make gourmet meals, our friend had to take cooking jobs in quick-lunch diners, and in lesser restaurants. But, even though he eventually found that he could make a decent living in this work, he yearned for the big money—the money he saw his employer make.

What did he do? First of all he took an inventory of himself. He found parts of his life that he felt did little to contribute to the success that he had planned, but he also found that many things could be turned to his advantage. Next, he decided what he must do with the experience he had. He had married and could not afford the luxury of further education, such as the long, expensive training to become a highly-paid chef. Jerry let his mind wander and did a little talking to all kinds of people. He listened, evaluated, and stored all of the information.

Here's what he found: He was living in a summer community with a very short season—a little over 3 months. Then, he found that the men who owned the restaurants in which he worked (he had two jobs) both only worked three months, and spent the rest of their year in Florida—doing absolutely nothing but enjoying themselves.

Next, he began to investigate the most obvious possibility—start his own restaurant. A few fast calculations showed that he was going to need a minimum of $100,000 to open a competitive restaurant in this resort area. He was disappointed—but not crushed. Up until this point, he had never thought of a sum this large. But because he had forced himself to have an open mind, he decided that anything was possible.

And, indeed it was. He took a "trip" away from his ordinary and familiar surroundings and found a declining restaurant on a side street that he was able to pick up for much less than he had planned to spend to open a new business. His experience was similar to Harvey's and the dry-cleaning store: a low down payment and monthly payments from future profits.

With a few innovations, a good cleaning, and some hard work, our friend was in business. Now, the important thing to remember is this—he did exactly what he had been doing for most of his adult life—he cooked hamburgers, made tuna fish sandwiches and dispensed coffee. But, he found a place to do it where he could work only three months a year and live a life of ease for the other nine months. True, he worked hard during those 3 months, but it was worth it to attain his $100-an-hour goal.

Here's how it worked out. . . .

- He worked 10 hours a day—6 days a week for only three months. A total of 720 hours.
- He made $10,000 profit per season.
- This worked out to nearly $14 dollars an hour—not yet close to $100 an hour. But, this success enabled him to invest in a fast-food restaurant franchise in a booming resort community, so that in time he was making better than $100 an hour for just managing the operation.

Earn the top rate because you are the boss

Even though you may be reading this book only to build a part time income, you will still be the boss of whatever you do. You do not have to do anything you don't want to do. And, you can pass over or refuse projects which you don't like or feel will not give you a proper return for your time.

This concept is very important. Many wealth-builders are willing to do anything for a "buck." They feel that it's all "gravy." Take our word—don't start out with this attitude or you will never hit the $100-an-hour mark.

Be selective—take only "outsize assignments" on which *you can make the most money*. Of course, if you really need immediate money, there is nothing wrong with taking everything that comes along. But, if you are seriously working toward your goal of $100 an hour, you must be very selective.

There is another important benefit from having this attitude. When someone wants you to do a job for them, they obviously will try to get the best work from you at the lowest possible price. It's only natural to want to save money. But, if you say no and that your higher price is firm, you will be respected as a professional whose work cannot be compromised. You may not get as many assignments, or jobs, but the ones you do get will pay you more for less work.

How to discover all you need to know to make $100 an hour

If you have made your self-evaluation chart, as we have suggested, you have taken the first step toward a $100-an-hour income. Now we want to carefully analyze the very specific work skills you have to offer. Don't limit yourself to those activities in which you have already made money. List hobbies and other interests which can be turned to profit making.

Once you have this skills list, place the activities in order of their importance to you—that is, put the one you like best at number one and list the others in descending order.

Now, make a similar list of what the money potential is for each of these activities. This may take a little research, because most people seldom realize just what a skill or hobby is worth when someone is willing to pay for it. For example, we heard of John T. who was a ham radio operator in his spare time, but not very happy at his job in an electronics factory. On a vacation trip to a Caribbean island, he found that all of the radio and TV repair work was being sent to Florida as no one on the island could fix a regular radio or the many ship-to-shore radios in the boats that were based there.

When he made his lists, he found fixing radios at the top of both, and he discovered that he could escape the drudgery of electronics assembly work and do the work he liked by opening a radio repair business in a very pleasant part of the world—a Caribbean island.

He too used a Power Shortcut. He was able to get the

people who owned the marina to assist him with both money and a place to work. He used the Power Shortcut of "people leverage" which is described in Chapter 6.

When he looked over the two lists he had prepared, most of the activities he liked and those he thought he could use to make money were near the top. By concentrating on these activities, he was not only able to look forward to fulfilling his dream of $100 an hour, but he was able to say goodbye to a dull job and to do the kind of work that he really liked.

So far, we have not given you any of the details of the Power Shortcuts, and this has been intentional. We want you to understand your needs and likes before you go on to your study of these "methods of the millionaires." This chapter has outlined the basics, and now you are ready for an in-depth study of the Power Shortcuts—formulas for success.

finding the good-luck magnet that is sure to attract success for you

2

Hardly a day goes by that you don't see the story of a self-made millionaire in one of the popular magazines or your daily newspaper. And, if you're like most people, you read the stories to look for the "secret"—the one ingredient that helped this person make his millions. Quite often the secret turns out to be something you knew all along—something that this person simply picked up and turned to immense wealth.

But, the stories you never read about are of those people who used the same, almost identical technique, and didn't make it. There are more people who fail than those who succeed. The "secret" of those who hit the big time is not only in knowing the secrets, but in minimizing the risks. This, then, is a very important part of every Power Shortcut.

We are not only going to give you the methods of the millionaires in the form of Power Shortcuts, but we are also going to show you how to make them work with an absolute minimum of risk.

What this will mean to you

1) You will not risk your future or your family's future by quitting your job before your wealth opportunity is truly working;
2) You will be able to experiment with different opportunities and ways of running a business without having the pressure of depending on it for your livelihood.

In the previous chapter we told you about Harvey L. who started his climb to wealth by buying a small dry-cleaning store. If he had quit his job at the beginning, it is highly unlikely he could have taken the risks necessary to make the business grow as it eventually did.

However, it is also important to understand that every activity will entail a certain amount of risk. We will show you how to keep your money risks to a minimum, but be prepared to risk your time and work to make a start toward your goal of making $100 an hour.

Keeping risks at a minimum

As we mentioned earlier, many of you will be reading this book with the idea of supplementing your present income. If it all turns out well, you will step out of your present job and go on to build a personal fortune. Even if you are in a hurry to get on with your fortune building, we urge you to test your way. Don't make the mistake of risking everything in one rash move.

If you approach your wealth-building program this way you will:

• Get a feel for what will be most comfortable for you.

- Be able to test the Power Shortcuts that most appeal to you.
- Build your wealth-building "muscle" while you are not under too much pressure.

This last point is especially important. When your back is against the wall, you will react differently from when you have plenty of time and no pressure. It is important for you to work at a level which will make the most money for you. Simply doing any kind of extra work for a few additional bucks may earn you some spending money, but it will *never* permit you to concentrate your energies to achieve your goal of $100 an hour.

When you don't have to depend on the extra money your early wealth-building activity will generate through the Power Shortcuts, you can develop a mental attitude that will be totally productive. You will find that your decisions are better thought out, and have a proper regard for long-term consequences.

This then is our main point: *stay at your present work* and test your money-making potential by trying a number of the Power Shortcuts. You will find that most of the Power Shortcuts involve the investment of very little money, so that you can freely try one after another.

How to find the right wealth path for you

Another important thing to remember in getting started with the Power Shortcut is to have a number of different projects in the works at the same time. Because you will be testing, and under little or no pressure, you should try as many wealth-building projects as your time and energy permit.

You may feel this is a waste of energy. After all, many successful people claim that one of the factors which led to their success was their sense of intense purpose—a singlemindedness which never let them stray from their chosen goal. Yes, this is true, but most of these people came to this singlemindedness only after they had tried, and often failed, in a number of different efforts. Former president Harry Truman had failed at farming and several other occupations before he became president of the United States. He had learned from each experience what to do, what not to do, until he discovered what he could do best.

Therefore, we urge you to try several things; dip into a number of activities that interest you and see which will be most productive and which will be most comfortable for you.

Then . . . after you have tested various ideas and found the Power Shortcuts which will lead you to wealth, concentrate all your efforts on this one activity. This will be fun! It won't be work, we assure you. It will be like visiting a bake shop and having a free run of all of the products. Taste this and that until you find what you like and then eat your fill.

By testing a number of wealth-building activities, you will benefit from both failures and successes. When we told you to take mind-opening mini-trips in the last chapter, we wanted you to prepare yourself for this facet of money-making. As you become used to experiencing new things, you will become more knowledgeable and proficient in making decisions.

How to use luck to gain a $100-an-hour income

Luck is an important element in every enterprise. People who are very lucky in some area will often say that luck had nothing to do with their success: it was hard work pure and simple.

And there are other people who work long and hard and never achieve any worthwhile success: often they will claim their luck is "bad." Actually, neither point of view is correct.

- *It is possible to improve your luck in any situation.*
- *Give luck a chance to work by trying many different things.*

This is the reason why we are urging you to try different wealth-building activities ... to develop new interests ... and to experience new things. All of these activities will give luck a chance to work to your benefit.

Another aspect of luck is *serendipity*. This is a big word, but simply stated it means finding success in ways you never imagined beforehand. Here's an example of how it worked in one case:

Alan C., a photographer friend of ours, ran a moderately successful studio years ago. It was successful because he worked hard, especially on weekends when weddings took place. When color portraiture was still rather new, he risked a lot of money and invested in the expensive color processing equipment that was required to make color prints.

Soon after, all the photographers in the area began offering competitive color portrait services. Ordinarily, you would expect that Alan should have worried about losing business. Not so. He found a way to make money from this situation in a way he never thought of originally: he went to his competitors and sold them on the idea of sending all their work to his color lab for processing. His competitors were delighted. They would not now need to invest in expensive color processing equipment.

You can probably guess what happened. In time, the color processing business was so much more profitable than taking pictures of weddings and babies, that Alan sold the studio and expanded his lab into a large-scale color processing organization.

This is serendipity at work. In this particular case, it worked again for Alan.

After Alan ran the lab for a while, many of his customers expressed an interest in improving the appearance of the normally glossy surface of the color prints. In the days of black-and-white portraits, people were accustomed to getting pictures printed on papers that had surfaces like "canvas," "tapestry," "silk," and other deluxe finishes. The manufacturers of color papers didn't provide color printing papers in such surfaces. So Alan got to work in his workshop and came up with an embossing machine to give finished prints these special textures and finishes.

A quick run through the machine and he could charge extra for each print. Here was a real money machine at work! Again, Alan found a way to make money in a way he never thought of beforehand.

But this is not the end of the story illustrating serendipity at work. Other photographers who did their own processing wanted a similar machine from Alan. He had two choices: restrict the sale of the machine and try to keep all the work for himself, or go into the business of manufacturing the embossing machine and selling it to photographers all over the country.

Alan chose the latter course and a wise decision it was, too. Again, in time the manufacturing business became so profitable that it made more sense to sell off the color lab and devote full time to the photo-equipment business.

Today, Alan has added many more items to the line he sells, both things that he has developed himself and items for which he is the exclusive importer. He's a very good friend of ours, so we are reluctant to ask what his hourly income is. It's a safe bet, based on his lifestyle, that it is many, many times more than what he earned working behind the camera years ago.

What is a Power Shortcut?

There is no magic in any of the Power Shortcuts—they are simply the carefully distilled knowledge of tested business successes. Each has been trimmed of the fancy language, the frills, and the details which make them difficult to understand. Each is the result of considerable work in the analysis of both success and failure.

These Power Shortcuts have been developed from the experience of thousands of businessmen. Their experience has been analyzed and broken down into its simplest form. Each is the nub of the matter, the important details that you will need to earn your goal of $100 an hour. But, make no mistake about it, nothing has been sacrificed to give you the strength of the shortcuts. Everything is concisely spelled out, in detail, along with the stories of those who have used them to build fortunes worth many millions of dollars.

A Power Shortcut gives you the leverage you need to build wealth

Perhaps you have heard the word "leverage" used by successful business executives, and wondered just what it meant. Leverage can mean different things in different situations. But, let's look at leverage in its simplest, most easily understood form. The best way to get an understanding of leverage so that you can apply it to the Power Shortcuts is to recall what an ancient Greek scientist once said.

"Give me a place to stand, and I will move the world."

Now, just what did he mean by this? Obviously, he was talking about a principle of science. With a long enough lever and a place to stand in space, even the effort of a single man could move the weight of the whole world.

Just what does "leverage" mean in business? Later, in

Chapter 10, we will give you the full story of Vernon K. who used leverage to start his climb to a great fortune. In a few words of example here, we will tell you that Vernon invested $1000 of his savings in an "option" on a piece of property.

True, this was limited-time option and Vernon was risking his $1000. But, for this amount of money he was able to control for a few months what happened to a potentially much more valuable piece or property.

Vernon's $1000 was really a "lever" because he used it to move a big deal. His whole enterprise is a classic example of the use of business leverage.

Leverage, then, is placing yourself in a spot where a little effort will do the most good. And, that's what the Power Shortcuts are all about. Power Shortcuts are the "levers" and "places to stand." Given any set of personal circumstances, you can put yourself in a position to do anything you want with leverage.

Think of the men who have done this—Henry Ford, J. Paul Getty, and Col. Saunders to mention only a few. They saw what they could do if they applied energy and effort at the right spot. And, they did something about getting to that *right spot.* So can you, and every Power Shortcut in this book will put you in a position of leverage. The value of this concept is that you can pick and choose from among many positions because every Power Shortcut is a different kind of lever to help you build your fortune.

Remember the statement of the early Greek scientist. He asked to be in the right spot, and he also asked for a long enough pole to move the Earth. The pole is at your fingertips with the Power Shortcuts so you can "move the world" in any direction you choose.

When you place yourself in the right position, and use the right Power Shortcut, you can accomplish great things. And, these Power Shortcuts will put you in a position to earn your dream—*$100 an hour for every hour you work.*

How to use power shortcuts
in every business venture

Making $100 an hour will require that you engage in some sort of business. You won't have to borrow a fortune and open a big factory to do it. You can, if you desire, start right in your own home. But, your wealth building activity will be some form of business in which someone *pays you for products or services*. And, as we have mentioned, this can grow to a full-blown business that you operate 8 hours a day, or it can be a part-time venture that you use to build your way to a full time business. Or, it can simply be an income supplementing activity to give you those pleasant extras that a paycheck never can seem to cover.

As a business venture, you will be faced with the usual operating necessities—financing, operating, advertising, selling, servicing, and all of the other management chores.

However, as you will discover, you will learn the shortcuts that others have developed by very hard work in their quest for wealth. You will profit from their successes, and you will be able to avoid the mistakes they made. And, perhaps most important, you will be able to avoid the risks involved so that you can head right to the top.

Our Power Shortcuts are not businesses in themselves. They are not magic formulas. And they are not a substitute for hard work. But, they are important techniques you can adapt to your individual needs. All are flexible enough so that you can select that portion of the Shortcut that will work for your particular project.

We want to emphasize most strongly right now that you are in no way bound to use these shortcuts exactly as they are spelled out in this book. Consider them as tested idea-starters. They will, of course, work when used as others have used them, but they are most useful in that they can be easily adapted to your own individual needs and ambitions.

Make success a habit

If you will recall the trip we asked you to take in the first chapter, we would like now to make another point on this same subject. When you took this trip, you *broke a habit*. True, your habit of driving to work exactly the same way each day may be a good one, but it never lets you take another view of your world.

The same concept applies to the Power Shortcuts. We urge you to look at them from different angles. If they work for you "as-is" all the better. But, if you want to make a change or two—to try your own innovations—we urge you to do so. Each Power Shortcut has been carefully selected from thousands of money-making business techniques on the basis of its flexibility. Each can be molded to your personal needs. But, before you mold them, you must try them one way or another. You must test each to see just how it can fit into your wealth-building system for attaining that goal of $100 an hour.

Each business situation has its own problems, and each requires very individual solutions, but when you read and understand all of the Power Shortcuts, you will be in a position to make the kind of smart decisions that will assure you a rapid climb to your goal of $100 an hour. In a surprisingly short time, success can become a habit with you.

Using the Power Shortcuts to cut 20% to 80% from the time needed for financial success.

There is an old saying—"Time is money." And, we're willing to bet that you have considerably more time than money right now.

Even though you may be working a long work week, and coming home dog-tired at the end of each day, there is probably considerable time available to you in which you can apply Power Shortcuts for your wealth-building efforts.

As we mentioned before, you are going to have to sacrifice some time to make your wealth dreams come true, but we're sure that you have never analyzed exactly what you are now doing with your time. We know first hand, because we did this a number of years ago and were astonished to find the time that could have been put to productive use—with a lot still left over for fun and relaxation.

Get out a pencil and figure out how much time you have for wealth building activities. Your list might look like this:

1. Free time available each evening after supper and before bedtime (skip some TV if you have to) .... 2 hours
2. Five evenings a week at 2 hours each equals .... 10 hours
3. Free time on weekends .... 10 hours
   Total wealth building time available each week... 20 hours
   Total wealth building time available in a year or 52 weeks............................. 1040 hours

Just for the sake of discussion, let's suppose that you have reached your goal of earning $100 an hour for these hours. Have you figured out what this will mean to you at the end of the year.

Save your pencil, the amount is................... $104,000!

"Out of the question," you say.

Absolutely not!

Let's say that you are willing to devote only half this free time available to your part-time fortune-building activities, and that you are also willing to accept only $50 an hour as a start. Here's what you could expect to make for only 520 hours of part-time work in a year: $26,000 a year!

Not bad. Most people would consider this a great salary for a full time job.

Let's be even more conservative, assuming that you are looking only for a small amount of extra money and still want to keep up with all of your evening's social activity.

Working 520 hours part time at half of the above amount, $25 an hour would yield you a tidy: $12,000 a year!

We could go on with the calculations, but we're sure that you get the picture. You can also see how it is possible to set your own rules, to control your time to make whatever you feel you want. But none of the above part-time incomes should be sneezed at. After all, very few people make as much as even the lesser figure working full time.

How to get the most for your time

There have been any number of books and articles written on the art of making the most of time. In fact, there are highly-paid consultants who spend all their working hours telling executives of large corporations just how to save time. But the essence of making the most of your time can be boiled down to a few simple principles.

Once again, time is money. And to make the most money for the least amount of time is the only way you will be able to achieve your goal of $100 an hour quickly. You must organize your activity so that every moment is productive. At first this will be difficult. The kids want you to play catch. There'll be a ball game on TV. And your wife will complain that you should be out painting the house.

But, you will have to get into a firm routine. Most people develop both good and bad habits exactly the same way. Watching TV and playing with the kids are not bad habits, but they shouldn't take up all your time.

At first, locking yourself off from the family will be difficult because of the strong pull of habit, but when you begin to see the money rolling in, you will quickly look forward to the hours you spend in your wealth-building activities.

Measuring the value of your time

We suggest that you keep a record of time spent on your wealth-building activities . . . and a record of exactly what is accomplished during this time. True, keeping these records will take a little time away from actual wealth-building, but it will be the best education you will ever get.

What you will discover, if you are absolutely honest in recording your time and progress, is that at first you will record a tremendous amount of unproductive activity. Then, as you become used to using your spare time for money-building activity, that you will get more done in the same time.

This is amply demonstrated in the case of Carl L. whose complete wealth history will be revealed in Chapter 7. At this point, it is sufficient to say that Carl worked in a chemical plant and spent a lot of time traveling to and from his job.

The pressures of the job, and fighting two hours of traffic each day, really took their toll of Carl's well being. And for all this, his income was probably never higher than $8 an hour.

Then, this lucky fellow decided to go into business for himself. At the end of the first year, Carl found that he was working harder than he had ever worked in his life, but was not tired, and was accomplishing much more than he had ever thought could be done. In fact, he is fond of looking back at his old corporate job and laughing when the fellow who replaced him makes the same complaints about being tired.

What Carl did was really very simple. He translated a love of fishing into a profitable fishing-lure business so that he now earns $100 an hour as a successful wholesaler and mail-order catalog house. His case is not that unusual, although even Carl will admit that it took him a long time to get moving. The point we want to make with Carl's story is that nothing will happen until you get moving with some idea or enterprise.

After a few months of watching your wealth-building time you will see a dramatic change. You may even be spending less time than you did originally on your wealth-building activities, and you will definitely be accomplishing much more.

You are now on your way to making $100 an hour—for comparatively little work.

This, then, is Power Shortcut number one: Set up a rigid work schedule; record every minute of time you put in and also record everything that you accomplish.

At the end of each month, we urge you to review your progress. Analyze what you have done, how long it took you to do it, and what you have learned and earned as a result of your effort. Actually, it will only be necessary to keep this record for a few months. After you see what is happening—how efficient you are becoming in your spare time and how much money you are making—the activity will become automatic. Then, you should drop the use of the time sheet. It was only a tool to show you what has happened to you, and how your habits have changed in order to attain your goal of $100 an hour. And, of course, once you realize what can be done with time, it is silly to waste it on this kind of elementary record-keeping.

Finding the best place to work

We have no way of knowing what kind of activity you plan, so it will be difficult to tell you just where is best to work. But, we have seen many self-made millionaires who make use of every spare moment, no matter where they are. We do advocate that you have one place to do the routine work—bookkeeping, letter writing, etc.—but it is important to make use of every minute of your time.

If you take the bus to work, you may read, doze, or chat with your seat-mate. Each of these is a pleasant pastime, but nothing more. And, if there is anything a wealthbuilder seeking the $100 an hour does not need is something to pass the time. Time passes quickly enough by itself—don't give it any help.

Think of what you might be able to do with that hour you spend traveling to work on the train or bus. Read important business publications, draft business letters, plan product development and expansions, and even keep your eyes open on the passing landscape for future business acquisitions. More than one person has written a number of books on trains while traveling to and from work each day.

This, then, is Power Shortcut number two: You must make use of every place—and every minute—to get your fortune building activities under way.

Use your home, your bus ride to work, your lunch-hour, your coffee break, and all that free time you have each evening and on the weekends. A list of places where you can work toward your $100 an hour goal will help to keep you on the track. It can be even more helpful if you list the specific activities that you can perform at each place. For example, if you are making a product, you would probably be unable to make it on your bus ride to and from work. But, you can rough-draft your letters and even handle some of your bookkeeping on the bus. This is the kind of organization which will enable you to make every minute work for you for your $100-an-hour income.

Using the Power Shortcuts without doing any of the actual work yourself

Once you get organized, and have the Power Shortcuts doing their best for you, it will be possible to have others do much of the work for you—often without spending a penny. This is a very important concept, and one which must be mentioned here, but one which requires an entire chapter to explain fully. In Chapter 6, we will give you the full story of how to put an important Power Shortcut to work for you—without lifting a finger to do any of the work yourself. This important concept is called "people leverage," and like the basic principle of leverage which we just explained, you will be able to place yourself in a position to have others do what you want.

Getting people to do your bidding is an important Power Shortcut and one of the most powerful you will ever use. The story of Robert F., to be told in Chapter 6, is one of the most dramatic examples of how one person can get others to do just what he wants.

In a nutshell, Robert scrimped and saved to buy himself a printing business. Once in business, he handled every detail himself, worked incredibly long hours, and found that business was grinding to a halt. What he hadn't thought about was his role in the business.

Robert was doing all the jobs he should have hired people to do for him. His excuse was that he was a perfectionist and nobody could turn out quality work like him. The result was that Robert had no time for the most important part of business—*getting business*.

For the first year, Robert's hourly income was *zero*. All the money he had saved and had borrowed was going down the drain, and he wasn't paying himself anything for all those hours of work. When he started using people to help him, that trend was reversed. When we last spoke to him, he was putting a good $50 an hour in his pockets and was working more normal hours. By the time this book is published we are sure his income will push through that $100-an-hour income goal.

How to use the Power Shortcuts to get all the money you need

Nobody hands money out at the drop of a hat. Furthermore, even people with the best intentions and ideas find it difficult to get the money they need and want to build an incredible fortune. Yet, some people easily find money when others find it tough to raise capital.

These lucky people have discovered the ways of harnessing money Power Shortcuts. They have learned that there is plenty of money around, regardless of what bankers may say, and that by using the Power Shortcuts covered in Chapter 5, they have been able to get more than enough money to finance their ventures.

Later we will tell you the complete story of Simon W. and how he financed his business idea with a powerful technique for raising money. As simply as possible at this point, what Simon did was to test his idea for a newsletter on a very small scale. When it proved out, he took the idea and the results to a printer and asked him to "trust" him for a much larger printing assignment.

The printer looked at the results of Simon's test, was impressed that it was a money-making idea, and gave Simon extended credit terms. Simon up-scaled his venture, and as you will see later on, he drove his income right through the roof—$120 an hour!

We're outlining this story at this point to convince you that all the money isn't in the banks, and even if a banker has turned you down for a loan, there is capital out there waiting for you and your idea if you know the technique for finding it. "Trust us" to show you how as you proceed through this book.

Whether you need only a few hundred dollars to finance some ads to get a mail order business going or you want a larger amount of cash to buy a going business, you can do it with the Power Shortcuts described later on.

How to make people want to work for your success

People like to be on the winning side. Contrary to the popular myth, not everybody roots for the underdog.

You may not have a going business, and you may not be wealthy, but it is still possible to get all kinds of people to work for your success. It is a popular experiment for beginning students in psychology to ask a group of people to rate another individual. Even though all of the people are given the same set of facts, their individual evaluations will all be different—some dramatically different.

What causes this? The individuals see the world from their own point of view. This simple fact can be used by anybody to insure that others will not only want them to succeed, but will actually help them to do so.

This, then, becomes the Power Shortcut number three: You can make sure that people will like you, and even work hard to further your success if you make sure that they see you as a winning personality.

And, this is quite easily done. Here are a few simple guidelines to develop the kind of personality that will make people help you in your climb to success:

- *Always be positive.* You can overdo this by being the eternal optimist, but a consistently positive attitude shows that you believe in yourself and in what you are doing. If people are going to do things for you, or lend you money, they want to be sure that you are the kind

of person who will carry on, even in the face of stiff odds.
- *Be conscious of other people.* Take an interest in *their* interests. If you have an interest in the things they value, they will like you and help you in your climb to your $100 an hour income.
- *Try to associate with people who are successful.* Not only will these people be able to help you with powerful contacts, they also are good for your spirit when things get rough.
- *Talk about other people—not yourself.* You will find that when you avoid talking about yourself and emphasize the good things in others, that you will be bombarded with friendships. People will also be much freer in giving you ideas which you can use in developing your wealth-building activities.
- *Admit your own faults.* This isn't easy, but it is one of the most important steps you will take in getting other people to help you in your climb to wealth. We all make mistakes. Not only will admitting your mistakes prevent your making them in the future, it will also show others that you are, indeed, a human being just like they are.
- *Build up the self-esteem of your associates.* When the people you want most to influence see that you are genuinely interested in them, they will be on your side all the way. You must be very careful here; it's quite easy to pull this off as an act of apple polishing. But, if you really take an interest in them and their activities, this should come naturally.
- *Believe that other people like you.* You will always have people who will not immediately like you. But, in

the main, if you assume that people do like you—and you in turn like them, your whole personality will take on a power of positive accomplishment.

There you have it—the concept of the Power Shortcuts, and how to get the most out of them. From here on in, we are going to be throwing the Power Shortcuts at you at a rapid rate. Each will be tied in with the themes of the chapters to follow, but if you have any doubt as to how they work or can be applied, it might be a good idea to at least scan this chapter again.

easy ways to smash the barriers keeping you from a big income

3

A famous sculptor was once asked how he had managed to make such a beautiful stone image of one of our earlier presidents.

"I simply chipped away all of the stone which didn't look like him," he replied.

What he was really saying is that every piece of stone has within it the possibility of greatness. All it takes is the removal of unnecessary rock to expose a masterpiece. And, this is exactly what happens to every human being when he tries to make the changes necessary to build a $100 an hour income. The potential is there for everyone to accomplish just about everything he or she may want, but first it is necessary to chip away the useless elements which stand in the way of success.

Fortunately, it is a lot easier for people to make changes within themselves than it is for a sculptor to remove pieces of stone. And, it is important that you recognize that it is possible for you to do just that—right now in your climb to the goal of $100 an hour for every hour you work.

Smashing the barriers to wealth

You may not be wealthy now because there are some very real barriers standing in your way. You may have put them there yourself, without realizing it, or others may have put them there against your will or knowledge. In most cases, it is a combination of both, but it is important to recognize that you have the power within you to overcome these barriers in very short order.

A barrier, in its simplest form, is something which stands between you and what you want. We are going to go on record right now by saying that most barriers are imagined to be much more of a problem than they really are. Consider, for a moment, those unfortunate people who have overcome physical handicaps to build fame and fortune. Franklin Roosevelt was a helpless cripple, but went on to be a very dynamic president.

The most important thing to recognize about a barrier is *not the barrier* itself, but *the way that you overcome it*. If you imagine a barrier to be a simple fence, and you are standing on one side of it wishing to be on the other side, you have a clear picture of what this kind of frustration can be. Now, let's see just how it might be possible to get to the other side of the imaginary fence.

- You might try jumping the fence.
- If you can't jump the fence, you might try climbing over it.
- You might consider smashing down the fence.
- Find the end, and go around.
- You can even dig under the fence.

One of the most frustrating barriers to a beginner in quest of making big money is the lack of capital.

"If only I had some money to invest!" is a common complaint. And most people in this position simply assume that because they have no money to start an enterprise, they are doomed forever to a low-pay, drudge-type job.

Not so! Here are a couple of people who made it without any capital to speak of. Each of them overcame an economic barrier in his own way. Their names are Harry D., an assembler in a local factory, and Warren B., who worked in the personnel department of a fairly large company. Neither man had an hourly income that anyone would be jealous of, but both had drive to succeed on their own.

Harry D., whom you will meet again in Chapter 8, discovered a way to make money one day while trying to fix his mower. No, he did not go into the landscaping business. Rather, he reasoned many people owned balky mowers and hesitated to get them fixed or tuned because local shops charged such high prices for even the simplest adjustments on power mowers.

Why not teach people to fix mowers and show them how to save money, and even possibly go into the business of fixing mowers? There and then a mail-order course in mower repair was born. But Harry had no money to print up these courses. Rather than give up at this point and say it took money to make money, Harry outlined his idea to a local printer. The printer was so impressed with Harry's plan that he offered to print the courses at his own risk. If the courses made a profit, he would take a portion of future profits up to a certain limit.

By smashing an economic barrier in this inventive way, Harry started on the road to a fortune. Later you will see how he attained an income of nearly $30,000 a year working part time. Easily, an income level of better than $100 an hour for the hours he worked.

Warren B., the other smasher of barriers, discovered an interesting way to make money publishing a directory. However, to sell the directory meant spending a lot of money on advertising in national magazines, and money was extremely tight in Warren's circumstance. What to do? Give up on a good idea?

Warren came up with an idea that enabled him to get more *free advertising* than he ever dreamed possible. The sure-fire, money-magnet letter he sent to magazines to get this free advertising is given *word for word* in Chapter 9. You're free to use it or adapt it in your own plan for building an income of $100 an hour.

Both of these are exciting examples of handling barriers to success. The important thing to avoid is just giving up and not trying to overcome problems standing in the way of your fortune.

How to remove the one obstacle to your $100-an-hour income

If you are going to build a $100 an hour income, you must decide that you will overcome all the barriers that stand in your way, even if it means breaking them down.

All of the ways of overcoming the barriers we have described can be thought of as direct attacks on a problem. While it is fun to imagine that all of us can do anything we want, let's be practical and say that this simply isn't so. But, a lot of what we think we can't do, is really quite possible.

Assuming that there are some things that just are not within your power to accomplish, there are other ways of achieving your goals. These approaches psychologists call substitute acts. They are things that you discover you can do that will help you to accomplish your goal another way.

What we have then, are two ways of attacking any problem . . .

- The direct attack.
- The substitute attack.

Either will work, but we feel that you should use the substitute attack only after you have completely exhausted all the possibilities of direct attack.

The direct attack is always the fastest way to get what you want, but as we mentioned, the direct attack may not work for everybody in every situation.

What is a barrier for one person can be a satisfying experience for another. Each individual is different and each sees barriers in different ways. Therefore, it is important for you, the wealth-builder, to be able to look clearly at the barriers and decide whether it is worth a direct or substitute attack. Many people have found that the things they considered to be boring or difficult actually turned out to be fun and profitable when they tried them. It is easy to sit back and speculate, but it is another to try hard.

Attacking the problems that keep you from success

Therefore, the next Power Shortcut is this really thorough checklist of dynamic ways to make that all-important direct attack on the barriers which are preventing you from getting everything you want.

- **Work with people.** And have people work with you. Very few fortunes have been made by hermits. True, many wealthy people appear to be loners, but they are really depending heavily on the assistance of others. Howard Hughes is a classic example. He kept himself hidden from the world, but can you imagine how many people he depended on to run his vast money-making empire? In Chapter 6 we detail all that you will need to know in order to make use of this "People Power Shortcut."
- **Don't give up easily.** This is probably the most common cause of failure. But, it is interesting to note that of the thousands of people who achieve great wealth each year, most

of them attribute their success to being persistent, rather than to any special talents or education. In fact, how many so-called educated people do you know who have described some very wealthy people as downright stupid. This example of "sour grapes" is just their way of showing that they lacked the ingredient of persistence.

When you develop the habit of seeing a job through to its successful conclusion, you will see very quickly that you will start looking forward to the next task which you had previously thought of as being unpleasant. In other words, you will be building the dynamic habit of success. And, as is often said, "success breeds success." Keep at it—don't give up. Each succeeding job will be less and less difficult, and you will find yourself actually looking forward to work that you previously considered a drag.

- **Be aware of risks.** But don't let them overwhelm you. At first, the only risk you will take, if you're starting your wealth-building on a part-time basis, may be the comments from your friends when you do not show up for a bowling night or some other activity. Their jeers can be easily fielded when you show them positive progress, if you stick to it as we have described above. This will be your first reward—letting your friends see the results of your activity. Then all the work will be sheer pleasure.

However, as your wealth-building activity grows, you will be faced with the need to take more serious risks. You may have to borrow money, invest money, and even decide whether or not to leave your regular job to devote full time to fortune building. However. you will see, as you continue through the pages of this book, we have tried to take the serious risks out of all of the fortune-building formulas we discuss.

If the risk turns out badly, don't let it get you down. Carefully analyze what went wrong, and be sure that the correct solution is permanently imprinted in your mind to prevent a similar occurrence in the future.

• **Always be thinking of new ideas.** Very few people will come up with the Hula-Hoop and make as fast a fortune as did the inventor of this toy. But if you are constantly thinking of new ideas—as they apply to your present fortune-building activities—you will always be in good shape It is the person who relaxes after his one flash of genius, hoping for future flashes, that will have problems. If you are persistent and are constantly aware of new ideas and new ways of using them, you will be way ahead smashing every barrier that can ever be placed in front of you.

• **You must train yourself to think quickly.** This is a lot easier than many people think. Most of the thinking you will do in your fortune-building activities will be in the form of decision making. Should I buy this machine? Should I invest in that franchise? Many important benefits have been missed by people simply because they didn't act fast enough.

Now, there is a difference between being *impulsive* and *decisive*. Being decisive implies that you have studied all of the available facts and made a decision in time to aid your growth to the $100 an hour income Being impulsive means that you make decisions on the spur of the moment, without taking the time to think about the consequences.

There is a little trick to be learned here, and it is this: If you know you are facing a decision, review all of the details well ahead of the time required for an answer. Then, mull over each detail at odd moments and you will find that the answer will come by itself. Your subconscious will be working on it, and the decision will be almost automatic. Your mind will work on the problem by itself, while it is still free for your regular day to day activity. Don't be fooled by people who tell you that they made fortunes by making snap decisions. They may have fooled themselves into believing this, but they have actually used this very powerful decision-making technique, often without realizing it.

One of the best ways of coming to a sound decision is to construct a "pro-and-con" table. This is what Tom H. did when he was confronted with the decision of quitting his job and making a start in a risky business, or playing it safe and taking much less money in the beginning. How he did it is fully revealed to you in Chapter 10. Here are the highlights:

Tom was earning about $6 an hour in a job at a food-processing plant. Working after hours in a part-time cleaning business, he was averaging another $6 an hour. (This was his first mistake: remember the advice we gave you about doubling and tripling your regular wage rate when working in your own business?). He was tempted to quit his regular job and work full time in his own business. The money was the same and he would be his own boss. Tom set up a table of "pros and cons." This is what it looked like:

> *Under PRO:* Tom listed all the reasons why he should quit his job and go into business for himself.
>
> *Under CON:* Tom listed all the reasons why he should hang onto a secure, if lackluster, job at the food plant.

Looking at the reasons written down in black and white made Tom choose the course of action under CON. He kept his job, but hired a helper to handle the cleaning business. This decision gave him a lot more free time, but less money, because he had to pay his helper. However, hiring helpers was the secret of multiplying his income. As he added people to his crew, business grew to such a point that he could quit his job with every feeling of success and security in a growing business of his own that had the potential of giving him $100 an hour.

Let's continue attacking the problems that keep you from success:

- **Make every minute count.** We have already gone into this in detail in the first chapter, so we won't take any additional space to go over this important concept. But, time really is money. After all, isn't the title of this book *How to Make Up to $100 an Hour Every Hour You Work?*
- **Keep your goals in mind.** Write them down and review them frequently. It is very easy to lose sight of your goals when you are immersed in the details of building a fortune. We once saw a very clever little cartoon on an important executive's wall which showed a man wrestling a ferocious alligator in a particularly murky swamp. The caption went something like this: "It's hard to remember that you came to drain the swamp when you are up to your neck in alligators." In other words, keep your eyes on the ball at all times.
- **Grow every day.** When you think that you are as smart or as successful as you can ever be, it's the beginning of the end. You must never think that simply because you have achieved your goal—$100 an hour—that you have reached the top. Once you're there, it will take as much work to stay there. If you follow the advice of exploring new things regularly, you will always be expanding your horizons, your personal outlook, and your fortune.
- **Ask for help when you need it.** This help may be something that someone can do for you, or it may be in the form of money or other tangible things that can aid your growth. It's not a sign of weakness to seek help—it's a sign of a smart fortune-builder who has realized that one of the fastest ways over a barrier is with the help of others.

Discovering the hidden wealth-building power within you.

Perhaps that sculptor we mentioned earlier could take a look at a block of granite and see a figure in the stone, but for most of us it isn't easy to take a look and see the potential we have inside us. Most of us see ourselves in terms of what we have already done and are now doing. But, man above all of the other creatures in this world, has the power to think and plan for the future.

Once your pet dog has been fed, he forgets about food until his stomach tells him it's time to eat again. But, we as thinking individuals can think about a meal in the future, even though we may have just finished eating. With these same incredible powers, it is possible for us to seek, discover, and use the hidden wealth-building power we all have.

Because you should be testing your wealth-building activities on a part-time basis, we want you to try a number of different activities—and to carefully think about how you feel when you do them. At this point, don't let a simple failure color your judgment. How many times have you hit some target the first time? Therefore, early success in a new venture is really not the most important measure that you will need to discover the hidden wealth-building power within you.

What we want you to do is to try to remember just how good you feel when you are trying something new. Try to get at these feelings while you are doing the job so that a possible failure won't make you change your mind. It's easy to be discouraged and rule out a potential money-making method because you fail at it the first time. But it is important that you get a strong feel for whether or not you like the work.

When you know what you like to do, there is plenty of time to polish up the skills needed to make it a success every time. The story of Ward L. can dramatically illustrate this point.

Ward had a routine job in a machine shop with a company that really didn't appreciate all he did for them. Ward decided that the only way to get out of this rut was to do something on his own, but he was working at a job that wasn't easily done alone; it required someone to employ him. Ward was operating a turret lathe in a production machine shop at $7.50 an hour, and simply couldn't get the money he needed to open his own shop.

Therefore, Ward decided that he would test his wealth-building capacity by trying a number of different things. First, he tried projects which were similar to the work he was already doing. He started doing repair work around his neighborhood, but found that his hourly income from this was about the same as his present job, and he really didn't like it.

When a friend suggested that he try expanding his hobby of photography into a money-making activity, Ward laughed.

"Make money at something that's fun," he said, "that just doesn't seem right."

But, he decided that it might be possible to do custom developing and picture printing for the serious amateurs he knew. He had a small enlarger in a closet and had been using it to print his own pictures, so he tried doing a roll for a friend.

In the middle of developing the roll, the developing tank fell, and the entire roll was spoiled. This made Ward feel that his whole project was useless. The friend for whom he was developing the pictures, instead of being mad, was very sympathetic and told Ward that he would give him his next roll to develop, in spite of the goof.

Heartened by this, Ward began doing this custom work for others in the neighborhood, and soon was spending all his time in his tiny closet darkroom. But, the closet darkroom soon became a full scale color-photo lab. Ward was still doing this when we last talked with him, and he was making close to $40 an hour working for the professionals who depended on him for quality work.

But, if Ward had been discouraged at his first failure, he might still be totally dependent on his machine shop job for money and personal satisfaction.

How to achieve the image of success

An image is something we see. But often an image is not real; it may fool us. But we do react to the image as though it was real. Think of the stories of people without water in a desert who run headlong at the sight of every mirage.

People will respond *to you as they see you*. If they see you as a quiet person, they will treat you in a quiet way and the same is true of all the other emotions. But, if you want to get the people who count in your wealth-building plans to help you, you must present an image to them that will say, "Here is a person who is destined to make $100 an hour."

Often, all that is necessary is what we and others have often called PMA—Positive Mental Attitude. When you see the bright side and are always optimistic, others will see you as a person who is working hard to build a well-deserved success. When you need their help, it will be there. But, when you let people see a side of you that doesn't give this image, you will often find it difficult to get their help.

Getting your picture in the paper

The image of success can be described in very direct terms as well. Your picture in the paper, along with a story of some accomplishment tells everyone that you are on the way up. And, believe it or not, you can have local newspaper editors run stories of your beginning achievements very easily. After all, newspaper editors have to fill up the columns of their papers every day, and often there just isn't enough news to do this.

If you have ever noticed some of the most successful papers are those which run lots of pictures of people—people are news and the editors know this. People like to read about other people, and particularly, they like to read about the successes of others. Many well-known magazines have been built on this tested formula.

This means that if you are on your way to building a business, whether full-time or part time, and can develop a "hook" for a newspaper editor, you will be able to build a powerful image for all to see.

The story of Claude R. comes to mind as a good example of this technique. Claude was building a part-time home-security business earning about $6 an hour in his spare time. He was watching people's homes while they were away. He would turn lights on and off at odd moments, put garbage in their garbage pails, and just generally make the watched homes look lived-in. But this kind of business is self-limiting. There are just so many homes that can be personally watched by one person. Claude was at his peak, but he still depended for a living on his full time job in a department store.

One day, a friend suggested that Claude tell his story to the editor of the local newspaper. Claude was reluctant because he felt he would be unable to handle additional business if others called as a result of the story. But, his friend insisted, and Claude dropped in at the editorial offices one day, and the editor was delighted with the story.

The editor gave Claude's operation a big spread, and emphasized that his service had actually resulted in fewer burgularies in the area.

Well, Claude's fears were confirmed; he got a number of calls from people who wanted their homes watched during vacation periods. But, he also got quite a few calls from people who wanted to work for him. Do you recall the word "serendipity" from the previous chapter? Well, this is an ideal example of serendipity in action. Claude got more than he bargained for—homes to watch, but he also got a number of people who wanted to do the work for him. By sharing the work with others he was quickly earning $30 an hour supervising his helpers.

The image Claude got from this newspaper article made him look a lot bigger and more important than he really was. But, in a very short time, his real image outshined the puffed-up image he had gotten in the newspaper.

This then, is the basis for a very important Power Shortcut. When you have a story to tell—even if it is only the beginning of a story—make sure that you get that story to as many people as possible. And, the best way to do it is to get a local newspaper editor to do the job for you. It's really quite easy; editors are crying for good material, and they will even write the story for you. You will never have to put a word on paper; it will all be done for you.

How you can make it big by joining the experts

What is an expert, anyway? An expert is usually considered to be a person who can perform some task with a high degree of skill. Whether a person is a tree surgeon, or a brain surgeon, he can be classified as an expert by the professional way he handles the job. And, he gets all the business he needs by being recognized as an expert.

A few years ago, diversification was the word in industry. Do everything; be in everything and the money will roll in. This idea ran smoothly for a while, but as these companies grew they also became very complex and unwieldy. Now, many of these same companies are returning to their old areas of expertise.

To be an expert doesn't mean that you must have a profession such as a lawyer or physician. It only means that you must be *the best at what you are doing* and that people recognize you for this skill.

Recall the story of Ken L. who worked as a plumber's helper for a number of years. As the helper, he got the dirty work, and the plumber got the big money. Ken never thought

easy ways to smash the barriers keeping you from a big income 79

seriously of leaving the job for better work because he felt that he simply didn't have the skills that his boss, the plumber, had.

Then one day, we asked Ken if he would unclog a sewer drain line. It was a snap for Ken, because this was just about all he had been doing on the job while his boss did all of the skilled jobs. We paid for Ken's skill at a very high rate—$45 an hour, you will remember.

In a flash, Ken realized that he, too, could specialize— and he could become the expert. He decided that as long as he could not make it as a plumber he would do what he did best, and that was to unclog drains. His boss, the plumber, got just as much money per hour for doing this work as he did when he did the more demanding work of installing and repairing plumbing systems.

With a loan from his family, Ken bought some second-hand power cleaning equipment. All told, his total outlay was less than $1000. And, he didn't need a truck. All of his apparatus fitted nicely in the back of his station wagon.

With word-of-mouth advertising and an occasional ad in the local newspaper, Ken was able to join the ranks of the experts. He was the specialist in getting plumbing drain lines moving again.

Now, here's the fascinating part. Ken's old boss saw how well Ken was doing, and began sending all his clogged drain problems to Ken, leaving himself free to do the work in which he was an acknowledged expert. This system of referrals spread, and now Ken has three trucks on the road every day and does none of the rooting work himself. The legend on the side of his trucks now tells it all—"Expert sewer cleaning." His income has reached the $100 an hour peak his old boss enjoyed for so long.

There is a Power Shortcut in Ken's story, and it is a very important one. Find your spot and become "the expert" in your area. Regardless of how inconsequential you may think it is, the chances are that your expert status will build a reputation and business faster than you can imagine.

How to make success a habit

If you've wondered why some people have a knack for doing everything right, it's because they have made success a habit. They are not "lucky" people, they have worked hard for their continuing success. Everything they do does not turn out right all the time, but enough of their efforts pay off so that they appear to have the habit of success.

You can do this by looking back at the things you have done successfully and copying them in the future. You can even look at the things others have done that have made them successful to benefit from their efforts.

Reading the stories of others is one of the best ways to build the habit of success. By now you have noticed this book is being written around the stories of success. We are illustrating the points we are making with stories which will not only inspire you to do everything you can to succeed, but also to show you where others have made the right turn to success. Publishers tell us that this simple fact accounts for the very real success of biographical types of books. Whenever the story of a successful person is published, it is almost always a success. People read these stories in order to find the thread of experience which will apply to their own lives.

By reading these stories—in this book and other books—you will build the habit of success very quickly and effectively.

A previous book which I co-authored entitled *How To Borrow Everything You Need To Build a Great Personal Fortune,** told many stories which will be of definite aid to those seeking to build the habit of success.

---

*Parker Publishing Company, West Nyack, N.Y.

We are strongly suggesting that you seek out the stories of success and adapt them to your fortune-building activities to build a consistent habit of success.

So far these first few chapters have been a foundation for the actual work of building toward your goal of $100 an hour. We hope that you have read them very carefully because in the next chapters we begin the actual work of building to your goal. The rest of the chapters in this book will take you, step-by-step, through the rest of the Power Shortcuts that will inspire you to achieve your $100-an-hour goal.

the 3-step formula that virtually guarantees you a $100-an-hour income

4

When you aim your camera at a subject, you are pointing it at something in order to get a picture.

When you aim a bow and arrow at a target, you are trying to get a bull's-eye.

Whether you are aiming your camera at a subject or aiming your personal sights on an income of $100 an hour, in each case, you must do something to get right on the target. With concentration, the arrow hits the bull's-eye; with the Power Shortcuts, you can hit your goal of $100 an hour.

There is another important point for your wealth-building in these examples. In every case of aiming, there is a conscious effort to get the job done—you have a plan or goal. And, if there is one thing that stands out in the stories of those who have made big money, it is the planning and setting of goals.

How to use the Three-Step Formula to attain your goals

To achieve your goal means that you will have to do something for money. You may perform a service, you may sell a product, or you may even make a product. But, whatever it is, first perform this simple test on your idea before you begin. It will give you an idea of what you can expect from your enterprise, and therefore, just how much money you can make from it.

Before we describe this important Three-Step Formula you should understand that if any of the steps shows that it will be hard for you to make the dollar goal that you have set for yourself, either reject the idea immediately, or consider just how you can change the idea to make the goal you have set. Don't change your goal.

Now, here is the Three-Step Formula:

need for the business + potential for profit + personal involvement = Success Potential

You must carefully evaluate each of these points before you begin your climb to your $100-an-hour goal. Fortunately, there are a number of Power Shortcuts that will help you in this task.

Let's start with the first—**Need for the business.** Obviously, you do not want to start a business for which there is no need. Yet, this is a common mistake many people make; they try to make their goal by doing something that appeals to them, but which does not have much profit potential. Remember, we said that your main goal *must* be the making of money.

But, how are you to know if there is a need for the business you have in mind?

To answer this question, begin by thinking of the things you need, the jobs you'd like to have done. Then think of why you do not have them, or do not have them done. Perhaps the cost of the item is too high for you to buy, or a service is too expensive for you to hire someone to do it for you. Can you make the product and sell it for less, or can you perform the service for less than someone else?

Ray R. found an opportunity for profit when he finally

faced the fact that his house badly needed a coat of paint. He called in several professionals and got estimates averaging $1,200 for the job. Overwhelmed by this figure, Ray wanted to see just how much of this was for paint and how much was for labor. What he discovered led him to the conclusion that here was a way to begin working toward his goal of $100 an hour.

Ray found that the cost of the paint was about $200, and the other $1,000 went for overhead and labor. His first thought was to do the painting himself and save the $1,000, but he soon found that painting a house in odd moments such as weekends and evenings would take all summer and leave him little time for fun. True, he might save the $1,000, but it meant a couple of months out of his life.

Ray's next thought was to find someone who might have the time and would be able and willing to do the job. His neighbor taught shop at a local high school and was forever complaining about his income and the cost of living. Hesitantly, Ray approached his neighbor and asked him if he might be interested in doing the paint job. After all, the teacher knew how to do it, he did need the money, and he had about three hours free every afternoon. Ray's neighbor jumped at the chance and quoted $400 for the job, if Ray would supply the paint. Ray was delighted and told him to go ahead.

One day, while Ray and the teacher were talking, Ray found out that there were a number of teachers in the local school system who were looking to make extra money and were willing to undertake similar jobs. Ray also knew from talking with his neighbors that there was a lot of painting work just going begging because of the high prices quoted by the professionals. It all clicked at once and Ray saw himself as a painting contractor who would never have to dip a brush in a can of paint himself.

the 3-step formula that virtually guarantees a $100-an-hour income 85

He went to all of his neighbors and offered to have the painting done at considerably less than the prices quoted by regular painters, using his house as an example of the neat work that would be done. He was soon able to get seven contracts from people within a local area, and hired nine teachers on a part-time basis to do the work. Here's how Ray took his first steps toward his goal of $100 an hour.

- Ray quoted and got contracts for painting seven houses. His quoted prices totaled $5,600.
- He bought the paint—at wholesale this time—for $450.
- He paid the nine teachers a total of $3600 for their part-time labor.
- This left him a profit of $1,550 after paying for the paint.

Now, here's the best part. Ray figured that he put in about 20 hours of time altogether to put these easy deals together, so he actually made *$77.50 an hour.* All he did was ask friends if they would like to have an estimate on professional painting at a cost much less than they had ever gotten—with no obligation. Hardly anyone turned this offer down. He then had the teachers visit the homes and give him the estimate of what they would charge—Ray, in turn, marked up the estimates, made the contracts with the home owners, and bought the paint.

He also spent 2 hours tracking down a paint wholesaler who would give him the best price. He saved a bundle here—almost 30% over retail according to his estimates.

Now, within this success story there are a number of Power Shortcuts that Ray used. Let's look at each.

Power Shortcut: Get orders, or contracts, before you invest any money.

Ray had a handful of painting contracts before he spent a

dime on paint. With the contracts in hand he was able to swing a deal with a paint supplier for a hefty discount.

Power Shortcut: Get the kind of terms that mean you will never have to lay out cash.

With these contracts, Ray was able to convince the paint supplier to give him 60 days to pay for the paint. Actually, Ray had planned to have all jobs done before this, but he felt that he might need this margin in case of bad weather. When the jobs were done, Ray collected his money from the home owners, paid the moonlighting painters and his paint supplier. He never played with a dime of his savings, yet made $1,550 or $77.50 an hour for his efforts.

Power Shortcut: Operate from your home.

Apart from the fact that it is quite comfortable to work from your home, there are a number of very definite business advantages to be gained. Others who rent office space must pay rent. When you operate from home, you save rent and can take off a portion of your home expenses from your taxes. The government, in effect, is helping you in the financing of your home business.

Power Shortcut: Keep costs down by hiring moonlighters.

Exactly what is a "moonlighter"? You can find them everyplace. Basically, a moonlighter is a person who needs extra money and is willing to work for it after hours from his regular job. You've known policemen who take jobs as guards or watchmen, or factory workers who earn extra money pumping gas at night and on weekends. All these people are moonlighters, and generally speaking, are willing to work for you for modest hourly rates of pay.

Moonlighters can include teenagers who work after school and mothers who can't leave the house to work because they have small children to care for. All these people are resources for you when you need work done.

When you line up a job, call up your moonlighters and find out what time they have available and make your arrangements. You collect the money from your customers (like Ray did with the painting job), pay your moonlighters, and keep the rest as your profit.

After a while you'll find that you have an extensive list of moonlighters who are anxious to work for you. Keep track of them together with a brief description of what jobs they do, and *what you pay them.* To prevent problems among your moonlighters, pay people the same rate for the same job. You want to gain a reputation for fairness.

Power Shortcut: Find out first what not to do as well as what to do.

What this Power Shortcut is saying is simply this: Don't make the mistake of going into the wrong business. You don't need a crystal ball to tell what businesses to avoid. One way is to talk with friends who are running businesses of one sort or another. You will quickly get a feel whether things are going "up" for that type of business or whether things look bleak. Another way is to do some reading.

Almost every newspaper carries in its classified pages a column of "Businesses for Sale." We are not suggesting that you scan the column looking for a business to buy, but that you read this column as you plan your climb to $100 an hour in an effort to see trends. The trends we want you to look for are kinds of businesses being offered for sale more often than others.

For example, as we are writing this book, there are a high number of employment agencies for sale. Various business conditions are such that now is not the time to get in the employment agency business. This situation may change by the time this book is printed, but we are using this example only to show you how to use this Power Shortcut to save yourself a lot of headaches.

Power Shortcut: Find out what your competitors are doing by getting your name on their mailing lists.

If you are planning to enter a business which uses the mail for sales or promotion, be sure to get your name on appropriate mailing lists. If you are afraid of tipping your hand, you can have friends send in their names. You can even set up a company by merely registering the name in the local courthouse and then renting a post office box in the company name and using that name and address to solicit information.

However you do it, you will be kept up to date on your competitors' actions, and you can plan your actions accordingly.

Maximize your profit potential

The *potential for profit* is another important aspect in your planning and is part of the Three-Step Formula which you must use.

Fortunately, there are a number of Power Shortcuts which you can use to make sure your wealth-building ventures are aiming for maximum profits.

Power Shortcut: Aim at the middle income markets.

According to government statistics, there are more people in what is usually called the middle-income bracket than those who are classed as rich or poor. These people are generally hard-working consumers who account for most of the purchases in the country. Therefore, to insure that there is a great profit potential for your venture, make sure that you can count heavily on the middle income citizens to buy your products or use your services.

Power Shortcut: Avoid businesses with high labor costs.

Although we have already told you to use moonlighters, we want to take this a step further. Using moonlighters keeps your labor costs at zero unless you have work to do. There is a large pool of people who are willing to work doing simple jobs like painting and home repairs. But as soon as you get into a business which requires the use of very skilled or expert help you are headed for trouble. Keep jobs simple.

Power Shortcut: Figure how much you could lose as well as how much you could make.

In Ray's case, no matter how he juggled his figures, he would lose nothing. He didn't pay the painters until the job was done, and he didn't pay the paint dealer until his customers paid him. However, every enterprise is not always this neat. If you find it necessary to invest some money before you start, be sure to figure how much you could lose.

Let's now take a hard look at Ray's business. Although it may seem like a fool-proof operation, he still had the potential for some loss. Just for the sake of example, suppose that the paint Ray bought turned out to be defective, and that it peeled. If every house peeled, (very unlikely) here's what Ray could lose:

- Each home owner could ask for his money back or have the job redone.
- Ray had already paid his painters, and since the peeling was not their fault, there was no way of getting any money back from his painters.
- Let's say that the paint dealer agreed that the peeling was the fault of the paint and agreed to refund all of Ray's money—$450.
- Ray then would still lose the $3,600 he paid the teachers, plus his profit of $1,550.

This would be a lot of money, and while the chances are remote, it is always important to consider both the profit and loss aspects of any business prospect. Ray put no money into his venture so he felt the gamble was worth it. But to be extra safe, Ray got the paint dealer to guarantee the paint—in writing—to cover this possibility. It would also give him solid legal grounds for possible court action later on.

Personal involvement means fast profits

The area of **personal involvement** can also be handled with a number of Power Shortcuts. We are devoting an entire chapter later on to this important aspect of wealth-building, entitled *Using People Leverage to Help You Earn up to $100 an Hour*. It is loaded with all the Power Shortcuts you can possibly use to make sure that you will have to do very little of the actual work.

Turning the Power Shortcuts into longe-term investments

Each of the Power Shortcuts we have discussed in this chapter can be applied to just about any business or money-making venture you choose. However, it is important, as we have stressed, that you select your specific goal and make the earning of money your most important goal.

The Power Shortcuts, once used a few times, will become second nature to you. You will not have to refer to them as you build your life toward the goal of $100 an hour. When we talk with persons who have made tidy fortunes, we keep discovering this aspect of Power Shortcuts—in the beginning, you have to keep them clearly in mind. But as time goes on, the use of the Power Shortcuts becomes second nature. And, interestingly enough we've found that while certain Power Shortcuts seem very specialized toward a specific wealth-building activity, very soon these techniques can be adapted to other situations. As you read, therefore, try to see how you could adapt our Power Shortcuts for your own, individual needs.

Maximize your hourly income by specializing

Have you been in some stationery store lately? It's often hard to find the greeting cards and writing paper because the display shelves are cluttered with hi-fi sets and cameras. Many merchants are following the lead of big business and are becoming diversified. But what is the net result? Often a zero gain in income, plus increased selling problems.

Power Shortcut: Find a small segment of the market and serve it well.

The doctors who make the real big money are the specialists. The general practitioner, while certainly not poor, cannot hope to earn the kind of money earned by the various specialists. Therefore, until you reach your first goal, stick with your one objective and specialize in that.

You are now reading what is referred to by publishers as a "self-help" book. There are hundreds of other book categories, and most book stores try to carry a few titles in each area to satisfy the reading habits of many customers. Sadly, retail bookstores are seldom very profitable ventures. But, with specialization, a good profit can be made even here.

In a large Eastern city one enterprising man opened a bookstore which specialized in "self-help" and "how-to-do-it" books. This store seeks a small segment of the reading market and does the job very well. Reports in the publishing journals show that this store has been one of the most successful ventures in the field in a long time. Why? Because the owner discovered the need in a small segment of the market and served it well.

There is an important corollary to this Power Shortcut of

specializing. When you carve your niche in a very specialized business, it is always very hard for someone else to dislodge you. Another "expert" will have tough sledding trying to take away any of your business.

How to Pyramid Power Shortcuts for fast, personal profit

Don't think of the Power Shortcuts as single devices to be used by themselves. They are like parts of a jigsaw puzzle. Put them together and you will discover a big profit picture.

Take out a dollar bill and look at the famous pyramid on the back. In place of the eye at the top, visualize your money goals. Now look slowly down the sides of the pyramid. You will see row after row of bricks. In our scheme, these bricks are all like Power Shortcuts, each built on the one below and all ultimately leading to the money goal you have set.

You have probably noticed that the pyramid is very large at the bottom and contains only a single brick at the top. This exercise will help you to understand what happens as you add one Power Shortcut on top of another. The closer you get to your goal, the fewer shortcuts you will have to apply, and, of course, the less you will have to work.

When you hear some talk about laying the groundwork for something, this thought can be applied to your pyramiding of Power Shortcuts.

In the beginning, you will use quite a few to form the base. The next row will contain fewer, as will the next.

In order to make the most of this pyramiding, and to insure that you get to the top in as short a time as possible, use this wealth-tested checklist:

- Start right now with your wealth-building plans
- Stick with your present job until you have tested the Power Shortcuts that will make you rich

- Try to start a business which requires little or no capital
- If your ideas need money, keep the early investment to a minimum. (Chapter 5 tells you how to use the power of Other People's Money)
- Work at home, and keep your overhead as low as possible
- Make sure that the business you select has the profit potential and that you will be comfortable in it.
- Make sure that the business you select has the potential to keep going year after year

When pyramiding Power Shortcuts, you should always be ready for expansion.

Power Shortcut: Plan for expansion; don't let the business get out of hand.

Most people working with new ventures have very little time to plan ahead; they are often too busy taking care of the day-to-day money-making activities. However, you must set aside some time to plan for your business expansion, or you might find yourself unable to supply customers, or worse yet, a competitor might see this weakness and knock you off in a hurry.

When Carry W. started a part-time typing service, she planned only to work a few hours a day to supplement her husband's income. Typing manuscripts for authors at 60¢ a page, she was able to earn about $4 an hour. The $75 a week she earned was a tidy addition to the money her husband brought home every week.

But word of her skill and dependability spread, and she soon found that she had many more offers of typing jobs than she could handle. Rather than turn them away, Carry used the People Leverage Power Shortcut (described in the next chapter) to pyramid her earnings from a mere $75 a week to over $200 a week.

Carry lived near a large university where the professors were constantly in need of typists to work on books and articles they wrote. The same university also had a supply of business students who needed extra cash for their expenses. When Carry saw the demand for typing services grow beyond her ability, she ran a small ad in the college newspaper for part-time typists. She was flooded with answers, and soon had a reliable pool of typists to do the work for her.

Of course Carry was also making use of the "Moonlighter" Power Shortcut, the "Home Operation" Power Shortcut, and the "Orders before Work" Shortcut. It cost Carry nothing to run her business at home. In fact, she was able to take off a substantial figure for depreciation on her income taxes. She didn't have any labor costs until she had a job in hand, and she had an ample supply of willing labor.

By planning for expansion, Carry's money picture looked something like this:

- When she worked by herself, she made about $75 a week.
- When she set up her moonlighters, she was able to make over $200 a week after paying typing expenses.

And, here's an interesting note. Carry stopped doing the work of typing herself and began acting only as a typing broker. Here 5 hours a week running the business earned her about $40 an hour.

How to get free professional advice for the business you choose

There is hardly a field that isn't served by some trade magazine. Once you decide what business you want to enter, go to your local library and ask them to let you look at a copy *the 3-step formula that virtually guarantees a $100-an-hour income* 95

of *Standard Rate and Data Service*, or *Ayer's Guide*. Either of these directories lists all of the trade magazines published in the country. And, you can get a wealth of professional advice from the editors.

Power Shortcut: Get the editors of national trade magazines to supply you with business information.

Business and trade magazines, as part of their goal to get advertisers, do all kinds of research. They have in printed form most of the statistics any beginning wealth-builder could use in his climb to the goal of $100 an hour. Because you may in the future be an advertiser in their magazines as your business grows, the editors are often very glad to send you stacks of research information that can shorten your climb to wealth.

When you look at a copy of either of these directories, check the subject classification in which your business falls and note the names and address of the magazines and their editors.

Then write to each, outlining your plans and asking for whatever information they can supply to help you in your wealth-building work. You will be surprised at just how much information will come your way. This information will save you the many hours of hard work and frustration if you were to try to gather it from personal experience alone.

Use this checklist and you will be swamped with important information to help you hit your goal of $100 an hour.

- Get a copy of *Standard Rate and Data Service* directory of magazines. If you are planning a business in a consumer field, use the "Consumer Edition." If you plan to be in a business, trade, or technical field, use the business and trade magazine directory.
- Look up the section under the heading of the field in which you plan to work.

- Read the various publishers' statements as a key to the kind of material published by the magazine.
- Write down the name of the magazine, the address, and the name of the editor.
- Write to the editor, and tell him exactly what you are planning. Ask him for a media kit and a list of article reprints which might be available.
- When you get this free information back, study it carefully and use it to help you plan your wealth success.

Hitting the $100-an-hour target

The Power Shortcuts we have given you in this chapter will put you well on the way to hitting your $100-an-hour target. They can be applied to just about any venture to insure fast and profitable success.

In the remaining chapters, we are going to reveal to you other Power Shortcuts—the Secrets of the Millionaires—that you can use to hit your goal. The next chapter is laden with wealth-producing tips for using other people's money to foster your success.

Now, before you read the next chapter, pull out your little sheet of personal wealth goals and re-read it. This basic exercise will keep you on the track toward your dream of $100 an hour.

how to use OPM to shorten your climb to $100-an-hour income

5

How many times have you borrowed an odd tool to do an important job around the house? Just the other day I borrowed a valve seat-dressing tool from a neighbor. This little device polishes up the inside of a faucet to extend the life of the rubber washer. It's the sort of tool the average handyman seldom has around. But, it sure comes in handy when a faucet is leaking.

Money can be thought of in the same way. It's a tool, and there are people who have it and will let you use it. However, unlike the plumbing tool, you may have to pay for the privilege of using Other People's Money. But, for the person aiming at a $100-an-hour income, it becomes very important to locate, identify, and use all the sources of money for as little cost as possible. That's what this chapter is all about—*finding, getting,* and *using* Other People's Money for little or no cost. It can be done, and we will tell you the stories of people just like you who have used the Power Shortcuts to get all the cash they needed to start, expand, and even buy businesses.

How to make Other People's Money work for you

There really are two ways to make use of Other People's Money.

- You can borrow the cash, using any of the techniques described in this chapter.
- You can start and run a business without the fuss and bother of borrowing any money at all.

When you borrow money, you will have cash in hand and can do with it what you want. You may have to pay interest, or you may not, depending on which Power Shortcut you use.

When you start a business without borrowing cash, you simply make use of the money that other people have—without ever seeing or touching it. This may seem too good to be true, but the story of Simon W. will help put the idea into sharp focus for you. We're going to begin this story with a Power Shortcut; later we will give you the shortcut which will allow you to work with the money of others without ever handling it. This Power Shortcut put Simon into business, and it is important to understand the technique first.

Power Shortcut: Sell to businesses—not individuals—to get a rapid start with no cash in hand.

Even though a person might be interested in a product or service from a personal point of view, if you make it possible for him to buy it with company funds and use it for business, you will sell considerably more than if you tried to sell the same product to him as an individual. Many fortunes have been made by people whose products are "business related," but personally usable. These can range anywhere from a pocket calculator to a company car.

This doesn't mean that those who buy products with company funds are stealing from their bosses. These products are helpful to the individual in a business and a personal way.

In fact, many one-man businesses buy this way themselves. It's just a method of buying what is needed in the most practical way.

Simon sensed this, and decided that he could sell a monthly newsletter which rated the restaurants in his area and made recommendations based on food, service, and price. Obviously this information is important for the businessman who must entertain clients. It is also the kind of knowledge that an individual would like to have when he is dining out with his family. And, most important, it was the kind of a newsletter which a businessman could buy with company funds, use for company purposes, and still benefit from in a personal way.

Simon had a winner and he knew it, but he didn't have the capital to get it off the ground. This is where the Power Shortcut comes in that made it possible for Simon to start a business without having to lay out a lot of his own money.

Power Shortcut: Use the promises of others to get all the money you need.

Simon wrote a sample issue of his proposed newsletter and had a local printer run off a few hundred copies. He mailed these sample newsletters, along with a sales letter describing the details of his service to businessmen. The mailing was made to them at their business address. He was very careful to tell them *not* to send money, that he would bill them at a later date when their subscription would begin.

As each order rolled in, Simon had in his hand the actual promises of many businessmen to buy his letter. They had said, "Yes, I want to subscribe. Bill me later." These orders were as good as cash for Simon; they were "promises" people had made to pay at a future date. Here is what Simon did with these orders:

- He showed them to the printer and told him that he wanted to print a much larger quantity of the sample

and the sales letter—and promised to pay when he was paid for the subscriptions.
- He made a mailing to all of the businessmen in his area and received 960 subscriptions at $24 each.
- His total income was $23,040.
- He found that it would cost him $3 per subscription per year to service his subscribers.
- His advertising costs were another $4000.
- His total profit on the deal, with no cash from the start, was $16,160.

All it took were the promises of 960 businessmen to buy the newsletter to put Simon into the big money. Here's the most interesting part: Simon estimated that he put in about 20 hours a month on this project and that his efforts were netting him $67.33 an hour.

But, he was not satisfied with his $67.33 an hour and offered to help a friend in a distant city to do the same thing. Simon supplied the expertise, and his friend did the work. Again, they didn't use any of their own money; they started exactly as Simon had done a year earlier. The friend's letter was just as successful, and the royalties paid to Simon, along with the income from his own letter, gave him an income of $120 an hour. Not bad for a business which had absolutely no capital at the start and was built on the promises of others.

There are a number of other important advantages of selling to businesses. These are some of them:

- It can cost a lot less to sell to business because you will have many people in one company who can buy from you.
- You will have fewer collection problems when you deal with businesses than when you deal with many individuals.

- You can count on repeat businesses. If you plan your product so that it wears out, or is used up, you will get repeat orders from businesses.

There is another Power Shortcut which is dramatically illustrated in Simon's story.

Power Shortcut: Invest time first, not money.

In the last chapter we described many techniques for setting and achieving goals, particularly the goal of hitting $100 an hour. Simon's story has portrayed how it is possible to set a goal, invest the time—but *not the money*—and hit the big time in a hurry. After all, that's the only thing Simon did until it came time to pay his printer. However, when he was ready to pay the printer, the money was there. This important Power Shortcut can be applied to many businesses, and we feel that you, the reader, should consider it one of the Master Power Shortcuts in your climb to wealth.

How to make lenders want to give you all the money you need

The rest of this chapter will tell you how to get cash with which to build your business. If you decide that it is necessary for you to have money in hand and are unable to adapt the no-cash Power Shortcut to your needs, this chapter will help you get the money you need at little or no cost.

But, before we discuss the various ways of going about turning up thousands of wealth-building dollars, we want you to understand how to use a system which will insure that you put your best foot forward when you approach someone for a loan.

This system works with anyone—the banker, the savings and loan man, friends and relatives. In fact, it works so well with all kinds of people who are in positions to help you that we have called it the P.R.O.F.I.T. system. You will profit, and the people who help you with the cash will also profit. It's a system that gives any lender an instant picture of your potential for making a fortune. Here's how it works:

THE P.R.O.F.I.T. SYSTEM

- **P** stands for Personal qualities. When you seek to borrow money, people will want to know what kind of a person you are. A careful examination of your personal qualities, carefully listed on a piece of paper will help those with the money to evaluate you on this score. Tell them about your abilities, what you can do, what you have done, and what you plan to do. If you have ever borrowed money before, be sure to tell them how quickly it was repaid. If possible, you might even consider offering references of those who have loaned you money in the past.
- **R** is the Reason you want the money. A simple direct statement, with a few details to back up the statements is all that is important here. If you are starting a business from scratch, describe it, and what you think it will be in a year or two. You might include a statement as to why you selected this person or company as a source of money. Perhaps you consider this person more astute and able to understand your ideas. Perhaps you have admired the judgment and business skills of this person, and feel that he is just the one to help you with the financing. This is not the old "butter-up," it's just good business.
- **O** is the Offer. What is in it for the person who is going to lend you the money? Here you must be specific. Are you going to pay interest? If so, how much? Are you going to offer a percentage of profits? A percentage of the business? Will your investor become an officer in

your company? Spell this part out in very careful detail. When you consider that a businessman invests money—not for fun—but for profit, you will then realize that he wants to know exactly what he will get for his money.

- **F** is for Facilities. There are two meanings for this word in your P.R.O.F.I.T. picture. One will describe your personal facilities. How are you going to make sure that the project will be a success. And, how are you going to make sure that the person who lends you money will not only get it back, but will profit as well.

The other meaning of the word has to do with the facilities of the business itself. You may be working from your home, and you may have certain equipment with which to make money. Describe these facilities and how they will make money for you and for the lender.

- **I** is for Insurance. Again, there are two meanings for this word. One might be the literal interpretation of the word—do you have insurance on yourself? Many investors ask for a low-cost term insurance policy on their clients to insure against accidents which would make it impossible for the loan to be repaid. These policies are seldom expensive, and any competent insurance man can give you the details.

The second meaning of the word involves the kind of safety features you have built into the deal to protect the investors. This might involve the product, in that you must make sure that someone else won't undersell you and leave you high and dry. It might involve the long term nature of the business. Is this the kind of business which will make money for long periods of time, or will it wear out quickly? All of these questions, when properly answered, will "insure" that you are a

man of your word and a man who can be trusted with large sums of money.
- **T** stands for Time. How much time will you put in the business? How much time will have to pass before your investor will make money? And will your investor have to put time as well as money in your operation? The best way to handle the time question is to make a calendar of events which will tell when everything will take place.

What you now have is called a "prospectus" by the top money people. In addition to helping you put together all of the information that will be needed by a lender, the P.R.O.F.I.T. checklist will help you to rehearse your proposal. It will actually serve as a script when you talk to the people who have the money you want.

How to have instant cash when you need it

How would you like to be able to write a check today for an amount beyond that which is now in your bank account? If you have any kind of history with a bank, you can have a short talk with your banker and he will let you reserve money, at no charge, for you to use whenever you want. You only pay when you use it, and the money is always held ready for your personal use. This is the next Power Shortcut.

Power Shortcut: Use "Ready Reserve" to have money ready any time you need it.

Ready Reserve will not only put money at your disposal whenever you need it, but it will also eliminate the need to face the banker every time you want to use his money. Here's all you have to do:

- Visit the bank where you have an account.

- Tell the banker that you want to set up a ready reserve for your own personal use.
- You and the banker will discuss the amount of money that he will set aside for your use.
- Once you decide on the amount, you can write a check, even if you have no cash in the account at the time, for the amount of reserve set aside for you.
- You will pay absolutely nothing to reserve the money. You pay only when the money is used.

You must, of course pay back the money you borrow this way, but it is easy. Regulations vary from state to state, but for the most part ready reserve accounts work something like this.

- You will begin paying back the money one month after you write the check.
- You can space out the payments almost to suit your needs. As a rule, you can take up to 20 months to pay back the money, and then you only have to pay 1/20 of the loan each month. You will also have to pay interest on the unpaid balance. The interest may be higher than some other types of loans, but it can often be worth it to have the money when you want it, without the fuss of talking to your banker each time.

21 common and not so common money sources you can tap

Don't make the mistake of thinking that the only one with money to lend is a banker. The truly aggressive wealth-builder will make use of every possible source, and this checklist can be your guide to loans that you never thought possible.

1. *Colleges and schools.* This little-known source of

money can provide you with vast amounts of money if you have the right approach. Wealthy people often leave money to schools with the stipulation that it be used or invested in ventures that will turn a profit. The schools get the interest from these loans, but are not allowed to spend the money on school projects. You may have a better chance of getting money from schools if your ideas relate to such school related projects as book publishing and training equipment.

2. *Private investment groups*. Professionals such as doctors and dentists often band together to pool their money for worthwhile investments. These men are often willing to try more speculative ventures than the more conservative banks and commercial lending institutions. They seldom advertise their investment activities, but you can find out who is doing what by talking with your doctor or dentist. If he hasn't thought of it, you might start the wheels turning and be the first one to tap a great source of money.

3. *Your suppliers*. The companies from whom you buy products and services are often willing to help with loans or extend terms on money you already owe them.

4. *Charities and foundations*. These groups often have money available to help aspiring fortune builders, especially if your projects relate to their activities.

5. *State development commissions*. Many states are trying to encourage new businesses and will offer, in addition to favorable taxes, money or facilities to help you get started. The local chamber of commerce is the best source of information on this.

6. *Small Business Investment Companies.* Called SBIC's by the money people, these companies do nothing but lend money to companies which they feel will make a good profit. Often, they will take a small interest in your company for their help. Look them up in the telephone book under "Investment Services."

7. *Small Business Administration.* This agency of the government guarantees loans for approved business ventures. Get the details at the local SBA office, which is usually located in your county seat.

8. *Savings and Loan Associations.* Although their main business is home loans, you can often get money for related projects such as the purchase of real estate. You can also use money from a savings and loan to buy income producing property such as an apartment house and land for development.

9. *Relatives and friends.* If you are on good terms with your relatives, they can be an excellent source of money. But, the family will know of your finances. Think about this twice before you tap Uncle Harry.

10. *Individual investors.* There are many individuals with money to invest. These people are usually retired or successful businessmen who have capital and management ability that they wish to put to work. You can find them by reading the classified pages of any good financial newspaper such as the *Wall Street Journal*.

11. *Pension funds.* When you work for a large company and it provides a pension for you, the money paid to you in your old age comes from the interest on invested money. To find out about an individual fund,

write to the "pension fund manager" and ask what kind of investment opportunities they seek.

12. *Investment clubs.* Employees in many companies often form clubs and invest their money in speculative ventures. The personnel manager of any company can tell you if such a club exists in his plant.

13. *The finder.* The finder is a person with contacts who can put you in touch with money people—for a fee. The fee is always negotiable, and finders usually collect from the person who *gets* the money. These people don't advertise. But successful businessmen often make extra money by locating money for friends among other friends. Ask everybody you know; someone is likely to turn up something, when a fee is involved.

14. *Factors.* A factor is someone to whom you can sell your accounts receivable. He will give you the value of the receivables, less a certain percentage. This varies from state to state, but it can go as high as 15%. This may seem a high discount rate, but it is a quick way to get money when your customers are slow to pay.

15. *Insurance companies.* Insurance companies use the premiums you pay on your policies for loans to businessmen. They can be an ideal source of long-term capital.

16. *The Veterans Administration.* If you're a vet, you can get up to $2000 for the purchase of equipment and for working capital. Details are available from the Veterans Administration, Washington, D.C.

17. *Mutual savings banks.* Most of the money available from mutual savings banks has to be used on home building and improvement projects. But, once the

money is in hand, you may possibly change your mind and invest it in your business.
18. *Leasing companies.* You can't get cash from these companies, but you can get the equipment you need without tying up large sums of cash.
19. *Investment consultants.* In addition to providing financial advice, these consultants often manage funds and can arrange for you to get the money you need.
20. *Industrial banks.* These banks do not offer the usual services of a commercial bank (checking accounts, etc.), but they can be a good source for business money.
21. *Other companies.* Quite often it is possible to get the directors of another company to invest corporate funds in your venture. Look for a company which could benefit from your product and service as the best possible choice.

There they are, the Top 21, the best sources of instant money. Don't stop when a bank turns you down; go on to the next source. It has been said that most fortune seekers don't get the money they need because they don't try all of the sources. But, as a reader of this book and a person who will have all the Power Shortcuts at hand, you should find it easy to get all the money you need in your climb to the $100-an-hour income.

How to get more money when you are already in debt

What is a debt? Money you owe someone is a debt, and depending on how you look at it, this can be the greatest asset you have when seeking more money. Believe it or not, many businessmen will often borrow money *when they don't need it!* They then pay it back exactly as stated in the loan agreement or even ahead of time. They do this for a very important reason. *When you don't need money is the time to build a solid credit reputation.*

Then, when money is needed for an important purpose, all you have to do is go to the bank where you had borrowed and repaid a previous loan, and you will get preferred treatment.

This, you may say, is great for the businessman with cash to play with, but what about the guy just starting out who is not in such a favorable position?

The answer to this is quite simple, and it involves the use of mortgage money and home improvement loans. As you know, a mortgage is really a loan on real estate—a building or piece of land. Let's see how Marty C., an $8-an-hour driver, took a $40,000 two-family house he owned and turned it into the money he needed to buy another two-family house for investment purposes.

Marty had bought the place some time ago for $40,000, putting 10% down—$4,000. This means that Marty had a mortgage for $36,000. The place needed work, but Marty knew that with a little money and some effort he could renovate it and get a much higher rent for the other half. So, he figured that with an additional $10,000 loan he could put the place in first class shape. He also wisely figured that when the renovations were completed, the old place would be worth more than the price he paid. In fact, he estimated, by looking at similar renovations, the value of his place would be $60,000.

With this figure in mind and the details of what he planned to do with the house, Marty approached a bank for the renovation loan. However, Marty asked for $12,000, feeling that the bank might give him less. The banker agreed with Marty that such work would indeed make the place more worthwhile, but he gave Marty $10,000. This delighted Marty because this is what he really wanted in the first place. This left him maneuvering room and leads us to the next Power Shortcut.

Power Shortcut: Always ask for more money than you feel you actually need. This will leave room for negotiations so that you will at least get what you want.

Now, with the money in hand, Marty proceeded to do most of the renovations himself, and he only spent $6,000 of the borrowed money. This left Marty with $4000 in cash in the bank, gathering interest. However, Marty really had other plans for this money. He knew of another building which he could acquire for $4,000 down, and he did this with the balance of the borrowed cash. This, too, was a two-family home and Marty had enough income from the two tenants in the house to carry it until he was in a position to do a little modernizing with the bank's money.

Of course, this modernizing left Marty with another bundle of extra cash and he has since gone on to even larger buildings and small apartments. For the time he spends on these real-estate deals, Marty estimates he is making $75 an hour.

This little story points up another Power Shortcut.

Power Shortcut: It is often possible to borrow money for one purpose, but later find a more profitable use for it.

These techniques will work for you—they have worked for thousands of other people in their quest for the $100-an-hour income.

Borrowing money is only one part of the quest for riches, and it is impossible to give every important detail when we have only one chapter in which to tell the story. However, the author of this book has a previous book which covers all of the borrowing secrets of the millionaires, and it is available from the publisher of this book. The book is entitled *How to Borrow Everything You Need to Build a Great Personal Fortune.* Not only does this book tell in detail how to borrow money, it also tells how to borrow, or have the use of tools, property, buildings and even the best efforts of highly paid professionals. The book can be ordered by mail by writing to the publisher, whose address is listed on the title page of this book.

6

using people leverage to help you earn up to $100 an hour

Everyone admires a self-made man, especially if he is a self-made millionaire. If you have ever had the opportunity to talk to these people as we do, you would come away with the unmistakable impression that all their successes were entirely due to their own "bootstrap" efforts.

They would like you to believe that you, too, can build success if you work as hard as they did. The success stories you read in magazines constantly emphasize this same theme of single-handedly overcoming great individual odds.

Don't you believe it!

If you want to make it *big* in any kind of enterprise, you have to understand and use to the fullest what we like to call a *master* Power Shortcut to wealth. It is simply this:

Power Shortcut: The less you work, the more you can get done, when you harness the magic of P/L Techniques

Show us a person who claims to be a self-made success, and we will show you a person who has discovered and is using these P/L Techniques—whether he realizes it or not. P/L Techniques are responsible for his fortune.

What are P/L Techniques?

P/L is simply "People Leverage." P/L Techniques are simply techniques you can easily master that will get all sorts of people working to propel you to your $100-an-hour goal. Just as a lever helps you pry open a stuck lid on a trunk, People Leverage is a force that you can use to open up all sorts of opportunities that would surely be closed if you attempted to do the job yourself.

> People Leverage—P/L—is learning how to use the efforts of many other persons to increase your own power and to multiply your chances for success.

You may ask, "Isn't it possible to make up to $100 an hour *without* the help of others?"

Our answer is "No."

"But," you say, "what about wealthy doctors with fabulous practices . . . attorneys who defend famous clients . . . or business consultants who command large fees for their services. Don't these people make a lot of money on their own without any help from others?"

Again we say, "Absolutely not!"

Look. The doctor utterly depends on many people you don't normally see: laboratory technicians, hospital pharmacists, X-ray technologists, nutritionists, and a host of other helpers all working as a team to help a patient get well. The doctor is the captain of this health team.

The lawyer has a staff of legal assistants and researchers who pour over law books to provide him the precedents and legal decisions on which he builds a winning case. The business consultant relies on a vast body of previous research that has been published in books, government reports, studies, and national magazines. Alone, he could never accumulate a fraction of the knowledge and information he must have to serve his client so effectively.

All these people, and many others, are using P/L Techniques to command up to $100 an hour or more. Most of them are using P/L Techniques without consciously giving it a name as we are doing here; but, after explaining the P/L concept to them, they've said things like the following:

"It took me years to discover this technique, and now it seems so obvious!"

"I could have been richer, faster, if I had known this secret when I started out!"

"It doesn't matter what you call it . . . I just know it works!"

There is no better way for you to understand everything we mean about P/L Techniques than to introduce you to our very successful friend, Robert F., who wasted a great deal of time discovering this secret by expensive trial and error.

Robert started as an apprentice to a printer and learned his craft well. The printing plant never ceased to excite him, even after he put in many extra hours of work on the presses. The hum of the press, the smell of ink, and the thought of profit constantly fed his one dream—to own and run his own print shop.

Robert worked hard and saved enough money to make this dream come true after some years. On the day he left his job to open his own business, everyone was sure that Robert was born to the business and would surely make it big.

In the beginning, it seemed as if every good thing predicted for Robert would come to pass. Within a seemingly short time, his press was running a full shift, and his reputation as a printing craftsman was growing in a way that made his competitors envious. This reputation was justly deserved, for Robert was a perfectionist and handled every detail himself.

In his quest for success, Robert saved money by doing a lot of nasty jobs himself. He cleaned the presses, delivered heavy skids of finished work, swept the floors, and handled jobs not requiring the skill of a master printer or manager.

Robert's standards were so high, it seemed he would never find helpers who would take the same interest in the work as he did.

Surely, a man with such drive and dedication to his work would prosper mightily. Yet, within another year, Robert discovered that the constant hum of the press had been replaced by longer and longer periods of silence. What had happened?

Robert's slavish attention to the details of his craft and the time spent working as a "janitor" in his own plant caused him to overlook the single most important aspect of his or any other business . . . *getting new customers*. Then, on the brink of disaster, Robert discovered the master Power Shortcut about P/L that not only saved his business, but made his original dream of becoming a success in a business of his own come true. He discovered the master Power Shortcut that enabled him to work less and get more done by using the magic of P/L Techniques.

Using the master Power Shortcut to reach your $100-an-hour goal

Here's a way of understanding this People Leverage Power Shortcut and fixing it in your mind permanently. It is vitally important you never lose sight of this important principle. Imagine your dream of $100 an hour sits on the top step of a long staircase. To reach the top, you have to climb that staircase one step at a time. *You will never reach the top step or get anywhere near it if you keep one foot always fixed on the bottom step.*

And yet, this is precisely what a lot of people insist on doing, and they never fully understand why success eludes them. In a nutshell: if you try to do all the jobs, particularly the low-level jobs in your business, it will be impossible for you to tackle the big, important jobs which you must perform well if you want to climb steadily toward that $100-an-hour step at the top.

In fact, the *less* you work on the small-time jobs in your enterprise, the *more* you will get done simply because you will be devoting *full-time* to the important decisions only you can make. This is the essence of the master Power Shortcut.

Putting the secret of the master Power Shortcut to work

Once Robert discovered that being a "Jack-of-all trades" in his business was no way to grow, he saw in a flash what steps were necessary to take his business out of the rut. Here's what Robert's new business plan looked like:

- He borrowed money so he could expand his facilities and hire several people.
- He hired a top-notch printing foreman who could turn out work that met his high standards. He was expensive, but worth it.
- He delegated responsibility to these new employees for day-to-day details which were keeping him from attaining his $100-an-hour goal.

Robert quickly discovered that he had time to go after new business. His new foreman turned out jobs that had Robert saying things like, "The jobs are as good as if I did them myself."

A young assistant that Robert hired took care of a lot of the odd jobs and prevented small details from growing into large problems.

Robert's reputation started to grow again . . . he added more and more customers . . . and soon he had his business loan paid off. By making the tough decision to spend money on help, Robert eventually made more money than he could ever have made working by himself. He used people to leverage his way to his goal.

This is the most important principle we want to get across to you at this point. To climb or to grow means you have to let others do more and more of the work—to free you for the really big jobs and important decisions that only you can do.

Smashing the barriers to a $100-an-hour income

In most cases, the biggest barriers to making up to $100 an hour are the ones you erect yourself. And, if you erect them yourself, you can certainly demolish them yourself! However, it is very easy to see mistakes made by others, but often difficult to discover these same faults in your own thinking. To simplify the process of self-discovery so you can eliminate the wealth-preventing problems that can plague you, we have developed a simple, three-step formula.

But, before we explain this formula, let us look at the barriers that Robert had erected unconsciously that thwarted his progress.

- When Robert first started his business, he felt an almost moral obligation to keep his expenses down as low as possible. Even as his business prospered in the beginning, Robert still hung onto these habits. He watched after every penny, and always felt he could do without employees who could share the work load.
- Even when Robert got to the point where he knew he had to hire help, he put it off because he felt he could never find the kind of competent, experienced people he demanded.
- In the shop, Robert's attitude was always one of "Let me show you how I would do it . . ." This reluctance to get out of the shop and out hunting new business

meant that his business was destined to stop growing. And, when a business stops growing, it starts dying.

From Robert's experience and near-disaster, we have derived our three-step formula which we call "The 3 Evil I's." You must avoid them at all costs. These are:

"Evil I" Number 1. "I can't afford outside help."

"Evil I" Number 2. "I can't find the right people to help me."

"Evil I" Number 3. "I can do it better myself."

We call these the three "Evil I's" because the person erecting such barriers to his personal success thinks of himself only. He is "I" oriented ... The surest way to rise swiftly up toward that $100-an-hour goal is to eliminate the "I" thinking that dominates so many business decisions. You must look at your business objectively and search out every area where People Leverage can help you grow.

Using many people to help you grow

Using people to help you grow is basic P/L—many people all working to help you attain your goal of $100 an hour. You use P/L Techniques to eliminate the growth-stifling "Evil I" in your business. Here are some hints on how to do it!

1. "I can't afford outside help." This is the first "Evil I" that every beginning wealth seeker has to face up to. We understand full well the problems facing a business in the beginning. You have to do all kinds of jobs yourself. The important thing is to remember that this must be a temporary situation on your part. Don't continue doing all the odd jobs forever. If you do, you will find yourself in the same boat as Robert, who lost all contact with new business clients.

Look ahead to the day when you can hire help. If you feel your business is of such a nature that you will find it hard to hire help in the foreseeable future, then you should think seriously whether this enterprise is worth your effort. To make your $100-an-hour goal a reality, your business must have the potential to grow and support a staff of employees.

You can often get free, or almost free help from relatives and friends.* Sometimes, you can bring in a helper who will work for a "piece of the action." In other words, you share a certain part of the business profits with him in return for his services. This technique is especially useful if you need professional services in your business such as a lawyer, accountant, marketing expert, or top-notch designer.

2. "I can't find the right people to help me." This is just an excuse for not looking hard enough. You have to understand that competent people are pretty much available *if* you know how to go after them. For example:

- You can advertise like any employer looking for help. In a competitive market, you will find few prospects unless you can make your offer outstanding. Try finding an agency that specializes in the kind of help you're seeking. They have the contacts and experience to attract people you never thought were available.

- Ask your suppliers to recommend competent people. Often, they are the first ones to know when a good man is seeking to better himself.

- Finally, you might talk to people who work for companies in businesses similar to yours. There is no law that prevents you from making a better offer to a man who is now working for your competitor.

3. "I can do it better myself." Nonsense! There is always someone in the world who is a bit more skillful or ex-

---

*For a fuller discussion of how you can get people to help you, see the description of using OPT—Other People's Talent—in an earlier book by the same author, entitled *How to Borrow Everything You Need to Build a Great Personal Fortune*. The book is published by Parker Publishing Company, West Nyack, N.Y.

perienced in any job in which you may consider yourself an expert. Actually, this is just another excuse that is used to hide the real reason for not hiring someone to help out. Usually, that excuse goes back to the bad habit of trying to save every nickel and dime because of the mistaken notion such frugality in business is good business management.

How P/L Techniques free you for big, important jobs

Once you realize that others can do work you thought only you could do, you'll find an enormous amount of free time to devote to the really important things you should be concerned with. These are the kinds of jobs that must be handled by you as the chief executive of your enterprise. They include:

- Finding new customers
- Searching out new markets
- Developing new product lines
- Cultivating sources of loans and capital for expansion
- Doing other important jobs.

Harnessing the multiplier effect of P/L Techniques

To this day, engineers are amazed at the Pyramids in Egypt and how they were built. Remember—these ancient people had no machinery to haul millions of blocks of stone, each weighing many tons, and then erect them into a structure that has stood for thousands of years. All this fantastic work was done with people. In fact, you could call this a classic example of the power of People Leverage. Each of the thousands of workmen added his bit of personal effort toward building this wonder of the world.

This bit of history can teach the sincere wealth seeker a very valuable lesson. It is simply this:

Power Shortcut: Incredible results are possible if you learn how to add the individual efforts of many people.

Let's look at how Tom H. adapted this to his own spare-time business. You will recall meeting Tom earlier in this book.

Tom needed extra cash to help him enjoy some of the things he felt were worth working for—a new car, a color TV, some money in the bank against a rainy day, plus a "dream" vacation he had been promising himself and his wife for far too many years now.

Tom started a spare-time cleaning business. He invested in a machine that cleaned rugs, drapes, and upholstery. It was hard work, especially since he had to do all the work during evenings and on his days off. But, he was building a business, and in a year he could look with satisfaction on a growing list of customers. Now came the time for the big decision.

Making the decision that builds wealth

Most men in Tom's spot would have done one of two things at this point. They would either stop adding new customers and consider their spare-time business a very adequate way to earn extra money or quit their regular jobs and then make their part-time business a full-time business.

Tom did neither. He chose the path to real wealth by taking advantage of People Leverage. Tom kept his regular job, but hired an assistant at the going rate in his area—$4.67 an hour. People said he was crazy, because most of his profit now went to pay the assistant's salary.

Tom figured he was making about $6 an hour profit when he did the work himself. Working on an average of 30 hours a week, Tom was able to pocket about $180 extra each week as pure profit. A lot of people would be content to let it go at that because they fail to see the power of P/L Techniques in a situation like this. Tom did see the opportunity, though. He analyzed his situation like this on paper:

30 hours of work each week @ $6 an hour equals $180 income (income is the same whether Tom or assistant does the work).

30 hours of work by assistant @ $4.67 an hour equals $140 expense.

Profit for Tom when assistant works 30 hours equals $40 ($180 income minus $140 expense equals $40).

This was a big drop in income for Tom in the beginning. Instead of having $180 extra each week, his income dropped down to only $40 a week. But, People Leverage had not yet been applied.

Well, it wasn't long before Tom hired another helper and bought additional machines. With two helpers Tom was pocketing $80 a week profit—again without ever doing any of the work! He was now within shooting distance of the original income of $180 a week when he was breaking his back after hours and on Saturdays to add this income to his paycheck.

At the end of two years, Tom had 6 helpers working for him, and he had some big cleaning contracts. Each helper was worth about $40 in profit to Tom, and that came to a tidy $240 a week. Not bad for a person who still held his regular job and spent perhaps six hours a week supervising his helpers. Figure it out: Tom was making $40 an hour.

Inevitably, the day came when Tom told his boss goodby forever. People Leverage had made him independent!

Climbing the P/L staircase to success

All along we've talked of P/L Techniques as a way of short cutting your trip to the top. Here is an easy way to see how you are progressing to the $100-an-hour step at the top.

Essentially, all the different jobs you do in your business have some definite dollar value. The dollar value of any job is fairly easily measured. Very simply, it's what you would have to pay to hire someone to do that job for you. Look at the classified pages offering employment opportunities. For example, what would it cost you to hire: a janitor or maintenance person . . . an accountant or draftsman . . . an engineer or a scientist . . . a financial director or a general manager of operations? There is, you will discover, a great range in salaries among these jobs.

Some jobs are worth relatively little. These are the low-responsibility jobs that persons with little training can easily handle. Yet, too often a person running a fairly substantial business insists on doing some of these jobs himself because he thinks it is just as easy for him to do it, or that there is some merit in saving the money by doing the job himself.

At the other end of the job spectrum are the really high-level jobs that should be the first concern of any person running a business. These are the major decisions involving the planning and directing of a business.

At a meeting we once held with some important businessmen, we explained this concept of applying P/L Techniques in all types of businesses. Immediately the hands went up; the question everyone wanted answered ran something like this:

"How do you know which jobs you should be doing and which jobs are holding you back from greater rewards?"

Our answer was, "Construct a job-elimination checklist."

You can build such a checklist yourself and you will be amazed at how quickly it can pinpoint wasted hours in your days . . . missed opportunities . . . and potential rewards when you fully appreciate the power of the P/L Techniques in freeing you for bigger and better things.

Power Shortcut: Hasten your climb to your $100-an-hour goal with a job elimination checklist.

We like to divide typical jobs into three general groups: low P/L, medium P/L, and high P/L jobs. A low P/L job is one that has a low dollar value if you paid for it. If you do such a job yourself, it is extremely costly because you are wasting time. You are wasting time because there are any number of other people who could very easily take over that task. If you consider every job as a springboard or lever upward to another and higher job, then this low P/L job has very little power to advance you to your $100-an-hour goal. You can find yourself stuck doing it forever without ever moving up.

On the other hand, a high P/L job is one you should be doing because the job is what running a business is all about—it's the important decisions only you, as the owner or chief executive, should be doing. These jobs are worth the $100 an hour we have been stressing. The job elimination checklist is our way of showing how you can free yourself from the low P/L job and work toward the higher P/L jobs.

LOW P/L JOBS (Jobs you should get rid of doing yourself as soon as you possibly can):

- Pick up and delivery tasks
- Cleaning and maintenance jobs
- Stuffing and mailing envelopes
- Shipping merchandise
- Every kind of "office boy" or clerical type job

MEDIUM P/L JOBS (Jobs you have to do in the beginning, but which you should plan on delegating to capable people as soon as possible):

- Accounting and record keeping

- Advertising and sales work
- Design and development on products
- Financial planning and budgeting
- Credits and collection work
- Those jobs normally referred to as "middle management"

HIGH P/L JOBS (Jobs you should be doing if you are serious about reaching your $100-an-hour goal):

- Planning your business growth
- Making important contacts for credit and capital
- Deciding on new lines of business
- Looking for suitable companies to merge with or acquire
- Making those important executive decisions only you can make

The preceding listing is only a small sample of jobs in the various categories. To derive full value from the last Power Shortcut—the job elimination checklist—you should make a similar list for your own work. Put down on paper everything you do, from the simplest task to the most responsible business decisions you are called upon to make. Now, sort all these tasks into rough groupings of low, medium, and high P/L jobs. If your list of low P/L jobs is longer than the other two, you have a lot of job elimination, or job delegation, to do. The point is that you should try to make your low P/L list *as short as possible as soon as you can*. It should vanish once you have mastered our concept of P/L Techniques. Your medium P/L list will take a little longer to eliminate, but you should strive constantly to shorten that list also.

Finally, the day will come when you are devoting all your time to only the high P/L jobs. We venture to guess, when that day comes, you will be earning close to your $100-an-hour goal.

P/L Techniques can assure quick success

Go back to our first Power Shortcut—the master Power Shortcut. People Leverage, or P/L Techniques as we like to call them, are powerful forces that can command quick success for you. When you learn how to use P/L Techniques effectively, success is virtually assured. But, you have to work at it constantly.

Therefore, we urge you to commit to writing your own checklist of job elimination techniques as soon as possible. Write it on a large sheet of paper and tack it up where you will see it every minute of your working day. This will be your ever present guide as you climb those steps up to your goal of $100 an hour.

how to earn up to $100 an hour working from your home

7

If you look at the classified employment ads in the newspapers, you will see executive salaries of $20,000, $30,000, and $50,000 a year. There are people who are killing themselves to reach these levels, while others who have never given the executive life a second thought are making hundreds of thousands of dollars a year right in their own homes.

Why, you may ask, do people work so hard to get these ulcer jobs? Why do they fight the crowds to get to the city each day? Why do they suffer the pressures of their bosses when it is really so easy to make more money and take less stress working in the peace and quiet of their own home?

Let's just take a look at that $50,000 annual income we just mentioned. This may seem like a lot of money, and the number of people who are paid by corporations at this rate is quite small. There are so many people competing for these jobs that the chance of your hitting this level is quite remote.

But, what does $50,000 a year really amount to in hourly wages?

About $24 an hour, for a forty hour week!

That's not very much, when you consider that it is possible to make up to $100 an hour right in your own home, without all the life-shortening strains of the executive life.

Get SMART—make a fortune in a home business

We're not flip when we say get SMART. We really mean it. SMART is a word which stands for the opportunities open to you when you start your own home business. Over the years, we have watched many people tackle home businesses, and have seen both failures and successes. However, those that have hit the big money have been in SMART businesses. As you have probably guessed, SMART stands for something important; it is a key word which will rocket you to wealth in a home business of your own. It's a Power Shortcut to wealth.

Power Shortcut: Use the SMART businesses to build rapid home wealth.

- S—*S*elling types of businesses
- M—*M*anufacturing types of businesses
- A—*A*ssistance types of businesses
- R—*R*esearch types of businesses
- T—*T*raining types of business

Years of research have shown that if a home business is to have a good chance of success, it should be in one of the five SMART categories. There are, of course, other types of businesses which could be run at home, but if you want to hit the $100-an-hour income quickly, you should pick a business which is covered by the SMART Power Shortcut. Let's look at each in detail.

S—Selling. When you run a selling type of business, you either sell something you make, or something someone else makes. If you make the product, you are also in the M (Manufacturing) category. If you buy and then re-sell the product, you are strictly in a *Selling* business.

This is a fascinating category, because you can sell many types of products so many different ways from your home. You may simply use your home as a base and travel to nearby businesses as a manufacturer's representative. Or, you may run a mail-order business and only leave your home to go to the post office to collect orders and the bank and deposit the checks.

If you decide to go into the mail order business, here are some of the benefits you will reap as a home-business wealth-builder:

- Mail order requires very little investment.
- You can do it all by yourself.
- You can operate anywhere. If you want to move, the post office will forward your orders anywhere.
- You can control it. That is, you can expand simply by adding products, or making more mailings.
- Mail order can be started part-time, continued part-time, or expanded into a full time fortune-building business.
- Anyone can do it. Age and health are not barriers.
- No great experience is needed.
- You can sell to anyone—businesses as well as individuals.
- Mail order is a very simple way to build a fortune.

The next chapter of this book tells you how to build a $100-an-hour income in mail order, so we will not give you the details here.

Selling directly from your home, other than by mail order can also be very practical. Here are a few ways this can be done:

- Running garage sales. You can run regular garage or basement sales, selling the products or surplus articles of others.

- Selling products door to door in your neighborhood, using your home as an office.
- Selling products to businesses by making regular sales calls on purchasing agents, and the like.
- You can sell products by telephone from your home.

To illustrate how profitable this kind of selling can be, we'd like to tell you the story of Doris K. Doris had an old barn in her yard and wanted to make money. To make the barn ready for some kind of business, she first decided to have a "garage" sale to clear away the accumulated tools, toys, and other "junk." When word got around the neighborhood, others asked if they might leave their "junk" for Doris to sell, promising her half of whatever the merchandise brought.

After the sale was over, Doris knew that the only thing she would use the barn for was to hold more garage sales. She would contact others who wanted to sell their surplus articles and take half of the proceeds for her efforts. Eventually, she began working with churches and other charitable groups, selling the personal accumulations of the parishioners and splitting the proceeds with the church.

Doris originally had no idea of what she was going to do with the barn, but this experience put her in business overnight and she now makes about $300 a week, right at home. She's only open Saturdays, and figures that she is making around $60 an hour for her efforts. The merchandise is brought to Doris. All she does is tag it, sell it, and collect 50% for her time.

M—Manufacturing. Don't let this word frighten you. You don't have to have a machine shop or a factory to be a manufacturer. To manufacture simply means to make something. And, there are many things which can be made in any home without the need for large amounts of space or special machinery. Here are the major points to consider when you plan to manufacture a product in your home:

- Simple equipment should be used.
- The product should be easy to make.
- It should be a product which does not require expensive raw materials.
- There should be a high mark-up on the finished product.
- It should be the kind of product that would not be attractive to a large manufacturer who might want to compete with you.
- You should be able to produce it easily.
- If help will be required, the product should be able to be manufactured with a minimum of skill.

Let's renew our acquaintance with Carl L., the fly fisherman we met in Chapter 2, who never seemed to have enough time to enjoy his hobby. His $8-an-hour job at a distant chemical plant kept him at the job for eight hours, and he spent 2 hours traveling to get to and from the job. However, in his spare time he did find a few hours to tie his own fishing flies and to use them in his very satisfying hobby of fly-casting.

Carl would spend his two hours traveling each day thinking of the lures he was going to make and the fish he was going to catch with them. He would also think of how nice it would be to enjoy his hobby more often. He often discussed this with a friend who was also a fly fisherman. One day, it hit Carl that he might be able to turn his hobby into a very profitable business. No, he couldn't become a commercial fisherman, but he could tie and sell his flies to other fishermen.

He talked to his friend, and the friend agreed to buy some of the flies. But this certainly wasn't going to make Carl a millionaire. However, Carl's friend mentioned it to others, and Carl soon found himself spending all of his spare time tying lures. Of course, as business grew, Carl had even less time to do any fishing himself, so he decided to take the bull by the horns and went into the lure business full time.

Carl scouted all of the sport shops in his area and started selling his flies to specialty mail order houses which advertised his products for him. He even recruited his other fishermen friends to help him in the work on a moonlight basis. Remember what we said previously about the benefits of using moonlighters.

When we last saw Carl's catalog of Wets, Nymphs, and Streamers, as these lures are called, he estimated that he was making over $100 an hour—or 20 times as much as he made at the chemical factory, and he was working quietly at home.

Carl sells a box of special flies, such as his Early Spring Selection, for $12. It only costs him $2 to make this collection. That's $10 profit. When you consider that the sport shops buy them in quantities of one to three dozen, it is easy to see how Carl hit his goal of $100 an hour.

A—Assistance. When you assist someone you can make money. And you can assist people in so many ways—from your home—that it is surprising that more people haven't discovered this secret of making up to $100 an hour.

When a woman baby-sits in her home, she is offering assistance and being paid for it. When a man helps a person plan a building extension, he is offering assistance. But, one of the most unique—and profitable—home assistance businesses we have ever discovered is that run by a man who bills himself as the home handyman consultant.

This fellow, Mark W. by name, has been involved in the building of many home additions, the cleaning of hundreds of sink traps, and the modernization of many basements. Yet, he has never dirtied his hands, and he wears sport clothes to the job every day. This is a home business with a wrinkle that has made Mark a wealthy man.

Mark has cashed in on the do-it-yourself craze by turning

his experience in maintaining and improving his own home over the years into an enviable money-making machine. After many years of being a do-it-yourselfer, the last thing Mark wanted to do was to become a handyman working for someone else. But, Mark reasoned, there must be people who want home improvements done and want to do most of the work themselves. He decided he could become a consultant to these "un-handy" people.

Mark offered to show people how to do whatever needed doing and to consult with them as the work progressed. He was also available at any time to help solve problems which would arise. But, Mark never lifted a hammer or drew a saw across a piece of wood. He was the planner, coordinator, and guidance counselor to those who wanted to do the job by themselves. His customers saved loads of money by doing it themselves, and Mark made loads of money by consulting with them.

Mark would quote on the entire job. He would figure what time would be involved and he would give his customers a written quote. When he told a person that he would charge $300 to supervise the framing and paneling of a family room, the customer realized that he was saving $700, since a carpenter would charge $1000 for his labor.

But, Mark knew that he would spend only a few hours guiding his customer to a beautifully finished job. Mark didn't supervise every nail and saw cut; he only outlined the work and checked to make sure that his "customer" was progressing correctly. He also answered questions when they arose, for the most part, by way of the telephone.

Even though Mark did not make exactly $100 an hour for his own time, he eventually recruited others to help him and made a profit on the time of his "staff of consultants."

R—Research. The business world is full of people who desperately need information, but either do not know how to get it or are unable to get it because they are just too busy. You don't have to be an expert in any field to gather this much needed information and make money with it.

Victor M. worked in an advertising agency and saw that his boss knew a lot about his clients' problems, but very little about the economic events which affected his own business. Often, Victor saw his boss make decisions based on very little solid information, even though that information was available and published through the year in all of the leading business magazines.

Victor saw a need and tested it. He wrote a letter to the president of every advertising agency in the country and offered to send, at the end of each year, a collection of all the information published during the year that was relevant to the agency business. Victor's price was $25, and he didn't even mention the size of the report, only that every important bit of news which would affect the future of the advertising business would be included.

The flood of orders was overwhelming and Victor was on his way to making a fortune. All he had to do was go to the library and scan every business magazine for articles related to advertising and make simple notes. When he was finished, he had a report that was 50 pages long. His customers were paying 50¢ a page. Imagine if you had to pay 50¢ a page for an ordinary 200 page book. It would cost $100! Victor made over $100 an hour for his efforts, but he also discovered another important secret that we are going to divulge to you as the next Power Shortcut.

Power Shortcut: Plan your business or product so you have automatic future sales.

Obviously, business conditions change from year to year, and the astute businessman must have information regularly on which to base his future decisions. Victor realized this when his customers began writing to him, asking when the next issue would be available. Obviously, he did exactly the same thing the next year and made another bundle. And, this brings up another important Power Shortcut.

Power Shortcut: Make the most money by selling to people who are already your customers.

When you have a satisfied customer, you are well on the way to the next sale with the same customers. Constantly trying to develop new customers is a hard way to make a million, but if you have the kind of product or service which can be sold again and again to the same person, you will be able to hit the $100-an-hour mark in a very short time.

T—Training. You don't have to be a licensed teacher to turn the Training idea into a $100-an-hour income. In fact, all it takes is a little initiative and an interest in something which others would like to learn to do.

Herman C. and his wife Freda enjoyed the hobby of ceramic making. They had a little kiln in their basement and would shape, decorate and glaze vases, mugs, cups, and bowls. They would give these handicrafts to their friends and relatives for presents, and soon found that many people were interested in learning how to do the work themselves.

Starting on an old pingpong table, and using their little kiln for teaching purposes, Herman and Freda told those who had asked about learning the hobby that they would give a course lasting 6 weeks. The class was two hours long and was given once a week for 6 weeks. They charged $30 per person for the course, and each student had to buy his own supplies. There were 20 people in the first class, so Herman and Freda hit $50 an hour immediately.

Soon, Herman and Freda found that they could also make money selling supplies. They contacted their supply houses, and bought in greater quantities, thereby getting an even greater discount. When they sold these supplies to their students at the customary retail price they made a few hundred dollars more with each group of students. Their $100-an-hour goal was not long in being achieved.

Herman and Freda stumbled on another very effective Power Shortcut in their $100-an-hour business.

Power Shortcut: Try to serve as many people as possible at the same time. You'll save time and make more money.

It was no more difficult for Herman and Freda to teach 20 people than it would have been to teach 5 or 10. Each paid his $30 and each sat and listened as the couple described how to work with ceramics. And, don't forget, these two moneymakers were able to work in their home, deduct the space used from their taxes as a business expense, and to deduct the fuel used to fire their students' and their own ceramic items.

There you have it—the SMART ways to make money at home, along with the Power Shortcuts which you can use to hit the $100-an-hour income.

How a business phone and some stationery can put you in a profitable home business

All it takes to be in business is a phone, a pack of paper and envelopes with your company name on it, and a recording of your company name at the local courthouse. Nothing more!

If you want to go in business with another person, you will do exactly the same thing, except your partner's name will also appear on the business certificate. You don't need a lawyer to do this for you, but if you want to start a corporation, which does offer you some legal and financial protection, you should seek the advice of an attorney.

Here's how to start your business for very little money:

- Go to the county clerk's office and get the business certificate application.
- Complete the form with all the required information.
- Sign the form, and if required, have it notorized.
- Pay the fee (usually less than $10).
- Get your new business certificate and you are officially in business. That's all there is to it.

Now, what can you do with this certificate to do business? Plenty, and all it takes will be the stationery we have mentioned. You can skip getting a separate business phone until the money starts rolling in.

Charlie L. turned his business certificate and stationery into a fantastic importing business in a very short order. He wrote to the embassies and foreign consulates in a major city near where he lived explaining that he was a manufacturers' representative and wanted to represent companies from their countries. The commercial attaches quickly replied to Charlie with lists of most of the manufacturers in their countries. Charlie then wrote to these companies, explaining that he was an independent representative and that he would like to sell their products in the United States.

These companies sent Charlie catalogs, and even product samples, so that he could begin making calls in his area. He offered to sell at only 10% above his actual costs plus importing duties and fees. Charlie could work at this small profit because he worked from his home and had no huge overhead to support.

Armed with orders, Charlie then used his new company letterhead to write to a few customs brokers and made arrangements with them to bring in the merchandise he had sold. Notice that Charlie was making use of an earlier Power Shortcut. He sold products that he did not own, and had not spent money for yet.

How to discover opportunities that need no space

Unless you plan to make something, or sell something which must be stored, you can have the best of two worlds—work from your home and not have to use large amounts of home space. Basically, you will work out of your "hat" as those who have made this a wealthy way of life sometimes call it.

Here are a number of ways you can do this. Some of them will not put you in the $100-an-hour category by themselves, but by combining them, as your time permits, you should be able to hit the $100-an-hour goal.

- *Act as a consultant.* When we told you about Mark, the home handyman consultant, we told you of one of the best consulting gimmicks we have ever heard of. But, there are others. For example, you can help others run garage sales. You can show others how to plan a party. You can even help those who begin a new hobby as a consultant.

- *Act as a broker.* A real estate man sells land and houses and usually operates from a very small office. You can do the same with many other things. Sam W. became a local delivery service broker. He found a number of small delivery services that didn't have time to go out and sell their services. Sam did this, and took a percentage of all the business he developed. Incidentally, millions have been made at this game by people who have sold space in ships and freight airplanes.

- *Coordinate the service of others.* Sally M., a widowed lady, found that she could make big money by working with the builders and contractors in her area as a service coordinator. She would get the right plumber or the right carpenter, for the right time, for each job.

She took a percentage of the job from each tradesman, and made several hundred dollars a week just by using her telephone.

- *Sell the facilities of others.* Beth S. was an enterprising person who lived in a delightful summer resort. The resort was covered with a number of small guest houses. Each guest house owner had a hard time attracting customers until Beth got them to work with her. She developed a combination rental business together with a service looking after homes for absentee owners. The house owners would give her 5% of the bookings placed by her. A few inexpensive ads in near-by big-city newspapers pulled all the guests she needed to fill the homes, and "moonlighters" looked after the homes between times for her. She now has one of the biggest homes in the area and lives in it—without guests—all year round. She makes up to $100 an hour and doesn't call what she does work.

Discovering opportunities that need no investment

Unless you are going to buy machinery, or products to sell, most of the opportunities we have described in this book require little or no cash investment. But, you will have to put in time, and, as the old saying goes, "time is money."

When you first get started on your way to the $100-an-hour income, you will have much more time than money. This is the time to invest in yourself by making the most of every money-making minute. The chances are that you can do almost everything yourself when you first get started. All it takes is time. But, this leads to the next Power Shortcut.

Power Shortcut: Make the time of others count in your climb to the $100-an-hour income.

When you have the experience of doing everything in your businesses yourself, you will surely be able to tell when the employees you hire in the future are pulling their weight. It may be an effort at first, but make sure that you know how every job is done and be able to do each job perfectly. We have a number of businesses going, and know intimately the details of each operation. If need be, we could handle every operation. Not that we do, but knowing when we are getting our money's worth is important in good employee relations and expert management.

Finding the right home-based businesses for you

When you decide to start a home business, you may be confused by the number of things that will appeal to you. If you are a photo hobbyist you might immediately think of a photo shop, or studio. But, this may be a crowded field in your area. What do you do then? This simple checklist will help you get the right start.

1. Make a list of every kind of business that appeals to you.
2. Using this list, pick out the businesses which you could run with the talents and abilities you now have. The best bets here are businesses in which you have previously worked, or businesses built on hobbies or experience where you have already developed some ability.
3. Using the Yellow Pages, find out just how many similar businesses there are in your area.
4. Try to find out how profitable these businesses have been for their owners. This is easier than you may think. Visit each business and pretend to be a customer and engage the owner in casual conversation.

You will soon be able to decide just how successful they have been, and whether or not the area could support your business.

5. Make a list of the expenses you will have. Include every item.
6. Make a projection of how much money you think you can make. This will be easy after you have talked with your potential competitors.
7. When you know the cost to start the businesses, the cost to run the businesses, and the potential, you will have a good idea of what the right home businesses will be for you.

From this basic checklist, we have developed several important Power Shortcuts to help you decide which businesses will be best for you.

Power Shortcut: To make the most money in a home business, pick a field where there are few competitors, or where the competition is doing a poor job.

It is always possible to enter a very crowded field and still pick up all the marbles. Marilyn P. did this in a small town that already had three beauty salons. These shops were located in fancy stores, and each had been around for a number of years. But, Marilyn opened a custom shop in her home and offered a highly personalized service—not the routine trims and permanents offered by the well-entrenched competition. She took a lot of customers right from under the noses of her competitors. And, this leads to the next Power Shortcut.

Power Shortcut: Even though there may be a number of competitors, there are always a few dissatisfied customers who are waiting for someone to offer a better service.

how to earn up to $100 an hour working from your home

No business can satisfy all of its customers all of the time. But, most customers stay with a business simply because of habit—not satisfaction. If you can pick off a few customers from each business with whom you compete, you will have a great start. When you know that you can take away a few customers from each of your competitors, you will know that the potential is good for your business.

100 ways to make money in your spare time starting with less than $100

There are more than 100 ways to make money at home, and the best, success-tested businesses and the details on how to start them and make them prosper are found in a previous book.* It's chock full of home businesses ideas that can be pyramided into your goal of $100 an hour.

There is one business which must be described in considerable detail, and we have reserved a complete chapter to give you all you will need to know to get started. This is the mail order business, and the next chapter will give the start you need.

---

*100 Ways to Make Money In Your Spare Time Starting With Less Than $100. Parker Publishing Company, West Nyack, N.Y.

how to make up to $100 an hour in mail order

8

Recently, we asked a mail-order millionaire friend of ours what secret he knew that made him so successful in this field.

He replied very simply, "I send people letters, and they send me money . . . lots of money!" This is mail order reduced to the utter fundamentals. What we will be talking about in this chapter are the many ways available that will have people sending *you* money . . . lots of money!

In no other field is it as possible to make up to $100 or more for every hour you work as it is in the field of mail-order selling. There are a number of advantages which are worth reviewing here:

- You can start on a shoestring in this business
- You can work from your home at any hour you choose
- You can draw customers from all over the world—they are never further away than your mailbox
- You don't have to worry too much about a big competitor putting you out of business. Your letter and his letter seldom will meet in the customer's mailbox at the same time.
- When you develop a successful offer, you can quickly pyramid your business by using the money coming in every day as an important source of growth capital.

No wonder so many people rush headlong into the mail-order business. Unfortunately, most of the people who go into this business seldom take the time to do their "homework" and to learn which paths lead to prosperity and which paths lead to ruin. In this chapter we will mark these two paths very clearly for your benefit.

Indeed, even if you decide not to go into a mail-order business you can apply many of these ideas to other types of businesses.

How to avoid the most common pitfall in mail order

One of the most common pitfalls in this field is also one of the oldest "con" schemes around. In fact, the author has a book printed in 1908 which gives a hilarious account of one young man's misfortunes with this scheme and how he learned his lesson and finally built a solid mail-order business of his own.

Basically, this scheme is very simple even though there are many variations. Some outfit offers a *pre-packaged plan* all set up for you. They have a good-looking product. An advertisement promises you everything you need to make "big money in mail order" selling their product. The outfit placing the ad offers to sell you brochures, catalogs, or complete mailing packages. You need to stock no inventory ... the outfit promises speedy drop-shipments to your customers. And, if you have no customers to which you can mail these dazzling offers, the people in this outfit will even supply you with "customer's" names on labels for a low price.

They tell you that all you have to do is to address the envelopes to these customers, pay the postage, sit back and await a flood of orders.

A little common sense at this point will quickly show you what is wrong with this scheme as a moneymaker for *you*. The obvious question is this: "Why does this outfit need me?"

If this offer of theirs was so good, they could mail all those packages or circulars to the customers on those labels and make all the money for themselves.

They need you to *pay the postage* and do all the work for *little or no profit.* It often turns out that the product is inferior, or that the list of customers names is very much out of date or full of names of people who have died, or who have moved, or no longer need a product like yours. Most of these mail-order plans will yield you a marginal return at best, or more likely, an out-of-pocket loss that will sour you on the real opportunities that exist in mail order. The first rule of success in mail order is to stay away from any pre-packaged plans that promise instant success. Success is very possible in this business, but you will have to build the foundations yourself.

How one person started a successful mail-order business with only a $20 bill

The story of Fred G. is a good example of a person building a solid foundation in mail order. Fred had a basement workshop where he enjoyed working with wood and making simple projects. He made some birdhouses of his own design and discovered a lot of interest when he displayed them at a local garden club fair. This set him to thinking.

Picking up some popular magazines in the field, he noticed that many of them carried page after page of classified advertising offering many different types of products and services for sale. Someone was even selling birdhouse kits. Surely, he reasoned, these ads would not run month after month if they were not producing business for someone.

Fred didn't realize it at the time, but he discovered the first rule of success in the mail-order business—a true Power Shortcut:

Power Shortcut: Find out what others are doing in the business, then copy them. There is always room for one more success in the mail-order business.

This is the hardest lesson for beginners to absorb. The most natural thing in the world is to search for a new and exciting idea or product that will make you a million dollars. A few people have done so, but they have been extremely lucky. But, if you take something that is tried and true, make it a little better, offer it at a better price, or give extra service, you have the makings of a mail order success.

Fred decided he could sell birdhouse kits by mail also. He placed the following classified advertisement in a garden publication which had a circulation of 125,000 readers:

> *BIRDS bring you money. Our wholesale birdhouse kits earn you big profits. Free details.*

With his name and address added to this ad, it ran 20 words and cost Fred a little less than $20. Then he sat back and waited.

With a circulation of 125,000 readers you might expect that such an ad would produce hundreds of inquiries. Fred was somewhat disappointed when the mailman brought him a total of only 30 responses over a period of several weeks. Actually, his experience was not unusual among mail-order users of classified ads.

Fred prepared a simple mimeographed reply letter that he sent to each of the respondents to his classified ad. He described his birdhouse kits in detail and gave simple sketches in the margins of the letter. In particular, he stressed that garden clubs, scout groups, nature clubs, and others could buy these kits at wholesale and then resell them at retail to members or others as a fund-raising means for the organization.

Out of 30 respondents, Fred was able to convert a half dozen inquiries into orders totaling $60. After deducting the expenses of the ad, the follow-up letters, and the material costs of the birdhouses he was making in his workshop, Fred had $15 left over for profit. Not much to show for all this effort? Wrong!

Fred discovered a workable idea that gave him a 25% profit on his sales. All he had to do was to pyramid this technique. This brings up the second Power Shortcut you should always keep in mind as you experiment.

Power Shortcut: Test ideas on a small scale. When something works, start your pyramid to build sales and profits.

As soon as possible after this experience, Fred ran the same ad in four other publications, except that he added a code letter after his street address. This enabled him to trace inquiries to specific magazines because he used a different code letter for each ad he placed. Some magazines produced more inquiries than others. He kept careful records of the inquiries that each ad produced. In addition, he kept track of the number of orders produced by each batch of inquiries.

Magazines that were unproductive, he dropped. Each month, as money came in, he placed more ads and tested new magazines. This brings up another Power Shortcut that every successful mail-order operator practices.

Power Shortcut: Complete and accurate records are the lifeblood of any mail-order business. Without them, you will never know if you're doing something wrong, and you won't be able to repeat things that you are doing right.

After a time, Fred was averaging over a thousand inquiries a month, and his classified ads were running in dozens of publications. His monthly gross ran about $2000, of which about $400 was profit. While not a fantastic business, you must remember that Fred was still holding down a full-time job. This extra money gave him financial "breathing room." No longer did he have to look after every dollar to make ends meet. He was able to put money away for investment in his growing mail-order business. Moonlighters were making the kits.

Fred had a growing list of customers. He also had a large list of inquiries to his original classified ads. This suggested additional ways of making money on his original investment in the ads that produced the inquiries. Here is what he did:

- Fred put together a special brochure of "sale" and "close-out" kits. These he mailed to the whole list of previously unresponsive inquiries. The fact that people didn't respond originally with orders did not mean that they were disinterested in his offer. After all, they were interested enough to respond to the classified ad in the first place. Fred was surprised at the number of orders he received.

- If people were interested in birdhouse kits, then it seemed only natural that they would be interested in other nature and garden items—bird feeders, bird baths, sundials, fountains, lily pools, and the like. Fred looked up some manufacturers and worked out his own arrangements for drop shipping orders to his customers. Soon, Fred was mailing a fairly large and impressive catalog to his prospects and customers at regular intervals.

Finally, after he had used his inquiries for his own offers, he let the names be rented to other mail-order operators through the services of a list broker. Without any work at all, this produced an automatic rental income that ultimately ran into thousands of dollars a year.

Again, without actually ever calling it a Power Shortcut, Fred was practicing the last most important Power Shortcut.

Power Shortcut: Once you have a customer or inquiry, keep selling. Look for logical additions to your product line and repeat sales.

This case history demonstrates the most important things you should keep in mind if you want to earn up to $100 an hour in the mail-order business. We will review them because they are so important!

- Copy someone else's success. Don't try to be a pioneer, especially if you have limited capital.
- Test all your ideas on a very small scale. Keep accurate records of every result.
- When you find something that works, pyramid your efforts upward.
- Don't be satisfied with a one-time sale to a customer. Keep going back to him with other offers. Rent your names to non-competitors for extra income.

These points are so important that we will spend time with each and go into specific detail so you can see how to apply them to your own quest for that $100-an-hour income.

The 100-postcard trick for discovering hot mail-order ideas

You can get the equivalent of a college education in mail order for the price of 100 ordinary government postcards. Remember what we said about copying other's successes? Buying 100 postcards will enable you to do important market research as a step toward choosing the right mail-order product for you to sell.

With the postcards, get yourself a fairly large blank notebook. It should have at least 100 pages. From one source or another, get a load of various magazines that run classified ads. Your public library probably has dozens. The magazines can be hobby, craftsman, garden and similar publications. Go through all the classified and other mail-order ads and answer each with one of your postcards. Most of the ads offer information; for the time being, don't order any products.

Each ad you answer should be "keyed" so you can keep track of the other operator's efforts. A simple way of keying such ads is to use a different set of initials for your first name: A. A. Smith, A. B. Smith, A. C. Smith, etc. Use a separate page in your notebook to keep track of each of these names, being sure that you paste the ad or a copy on the page for reference later on.

As the responses start rolling in, keep track of them in your notebook. Identify all the pieces so you know which piece came from which source. Not surprisingly, you will discover that most advertisers will send you more than one piece. Some types of products will appear more frequently than others. Keep a tabulation of products and services. If you get catalogs with a number of items, keep track of which products are repeated most often.

This will take some work, but every minute spent on this effort will pay you big dividends in your quest for mail-order success techniques.

After a while, you will start getting mail from advertisers that are not among your original list of ads. This means that the original advertiser is renting your name to other mail-order businessmen. Keep track of these mailing pieces in your notebook and you will discover how others choose prospects to which to mail their offerings.

After you've run this experiment for a while, you should have a good idea of:

- What are the most popular mail-order products and services.
- How to put together an effective mail-order selling brochure.
- How to price a product for a particular market.
- How to choose the right mailing lists.

This is an impressive list of accomplishments, and all it cost you was 100 postcards, a cheap notebook, and some of your time.

Deciding on a product or services to sell

After you have completed your 100-postcard market research experiment, you will have a good idea of what sells well by mail, but you will still have to make an individual decision for yourself. Here are some guidelines that should prove helpful:

- All things being equal, choose an area or product line that you find interesting or satisfying. A lot of successful mail-order businesses are built around some hobby of the owner.
- If you intend to sell a manufactured product, explore alternate sources of supply very carefully. Generally speaking, stay away from items available only from a single source, or those that have to be imported from a foreign supplier. Nothing is worse than to have orders in hand that you can't fill.
- Be realistic about the prices you can pay and what you can charge your customers. It is almost impossible to make a mail-order proposition pay if your wholesale cost is more than one-third the retail price you are

charging. In other words, you must get *at least* a 66% discount off list. Some suppliers offer a 50% discount as a great deal, but experience shows that it is virtually impossible to sell anything at such a margin and still make a profit.

- Many good mail-order items are seldom found in stores. Most successful are specialized items for the home, car, hobby, or business interests. Any item that can shorten some job in business is always a good prospect for success.
- The product should be easy to pack and ship. Beginners often overlook this point, and their profits are eaten up by shipping expenses. Check carefully the post office limits on weight, size, and mailability of the product. Fragile items invite a lot of headaches with claims arising out of breakage or loss. For this reason, books and other publications are good mail-order items—they are easy and inexpensive to ship and are virtually unbreakable.

Speaking of books and other publications, consider selling something that you can publish yourself. It is not as difficult as you might first think. Selling something you publish yourself has two great advantages as a mail-order item:

1) You can easily control your inventory. Print a small quantity as a start. If the sales zoom, you can quickly reprint to fill orders without delay;

2) You can generally charge more for a publication, compared to what it costs to produce, than for some manufactured item. Some people will pay hundreds of dollars for some special report that cost a dollar or two to print. People will pay well for information that helps them.

A fortune from Specialized Newsletters

If you are an expert in some area, or work in some specialized field, you may find that there is a need for a newsletter in this field which reports current events. It may sound incredible, but you don't need a staff of reporters to put together a very valuable newsletter. Most newsletters simply digest and reprint news readily available from other sources. People will pay good money for such a newsletter because it saves them the time of reading all the publications in the field. It is not uncommon for a newsletter of four pages that is published every month to command a subscription price of $50 a year.

Publishing a full-fledged hard-cover book may be somewhat ambitious (and expensive) as a start. However, you can publish 24, 32, or 48-page booklets at relatively low cost. Again, depending on the kind of information you are selling, you can easily get up to $10 a copy.

Mail-order courses are very profitable if you discover a need and can fill it. Harry D. discovered such a need one day when the gasoline engine of his power mower stopped working. A local repair shop gave him a quote of $42 for parts and labor to repair the machine. The mower only cost $69.95 at a sale, so Harry was reluctant to put so much money into repairs. Yet, it seemed a shame to junk the mower.

"What the heck!" Harry said to himself, and decided to try fixing the engine of the mower himself. A letter to the manufacturer brought him a copy of the maintenance manual.

Harry was no mechanical genius, but he had little trouble following the manual and fixing his mower. Total outlay: a couple of hours of time, plus $5.80 in parts. Looking over this satisfying experience, Harry came upon a mail-order idea that made him wealthy.

There must be thousands of people, Harry reasoned, who would like to save money doing their own small-motor repairs, or even to do such repairs as a part-time business. All these people needed was something to help them. Here's what Harry did:

- Harry wrote to the three or four major manufacturers of small gas engines and got their shop manuals.
- He got permission from the various makers to adapt this material into a short course in small-motor repair and maintenance.
- He added some material on how to start a motor-repair business. Basically, this was free material he picked up from the many free booklets available from the Small Business Administration.
- Finally, Harry went to a printer and explained his idea. The printer agreed to become a partner for a share of the profits, and would do all the printing of the course manual on speculation.

Harry ran a classified ad in a popular handyman magazine under the heading "Money Making Opportunities." The ad read as follows:

> MAKE BIG MONEY *fixing small gas engines. Low-cost course shows you how. Details free. Box XXX, City, State, Zip.*

He had a sales letter prepared which was printed by his printer partner. This letter was sent to every respondent to the ad, and out of 76 initial inquiries, Harry eventually sold 10 courses at $15 each. Here's what his income statement looked like after this test of a mail-order idea:

Total income (10 courses @ $15 each) $150
  less these expenses
    classified ad $20
    cost of replying to 76 inquiries $15
    cost of printing course ($2 each) $20
      Total expenses paid off $55
Total profit ($150 less $55 in expenses) $95

Harry previously agreed to give his printer partner one-quarter of all the net profits for taking the risk in printing the course before they were sold. This meant that Harry could keep $71 as his share. Needless to say, Harry did not stop there. He kept pyramiding his profits into more and more ads in more and more magazines until he was selling 300 courses a month. His profits were averaging over $2000 a month!

In addition, Harry was now getting about 3000 inquiries a month. At this level, he had no trouble in getting a list broker to take over all the maintenance of his list and to market it to non-competitors. List rental income added another $5000 a year to Harry's profits—truly an automatic income.

Considering the amount of time he was spending on his business, which practically ran itself, Harry's income was well over $100 an hour.

Developing a sure-fire formula for a successful offer

In the end, the only way to know whether you have a successful offer is to test it out in the marketplace. That is the attraction of mail-order selling—you can invest a very modest amount of capital to test the idea in the beginning. If the idea flops, you've lost only a little money; if it works, you can pyramid the idea upward.

However, even before you invest a small amount of

money in testing, you can do some things that will give you an edge on success.

Ask yourself the following questions:

- Is the product readily available in retail stores? If yes, then you will have a problem with people who would rather not wait for their merchandise. The best mail-order product is one that you can honestly say is available from no other source but you.
- Does the product or service promise benefits to the user, such as saving time, money, preventing problems, etc.? Good mail-order offers promise and deliver solid user benefits.
- Is the price attractive? Nothing sells like a bargain.
- Can you identify and locate potential customers for your product or service? For example: If you're selling a tool that is useful to amateur woodworkers, you have a lot of magazines and mailing lists you can use to reach these hobbyists. They can be identified. On the other hand, if you have something of interest to people who are planning on moving from their homes, then you will have a problem finding and identifying your potential customers. There is no way of identifying a person who is planning to move.
- Finally, and most important, no one will buy a "pig in a poke." An unqualified money-back guarantee is absolutely necessary if you wish to do business in mail order. Some of the most successful mail-order operators will even ship merchandise on approval with a bill which is paid by the customer only after he has examined the merchandise.

At this point, you should have some idea of a product or service you want to try to sell by mail. You've asked all the critical questions and everything is "go." What is the next step?

Two steps to mail-order success

You will have to decide whether you will try to sell by direct mail, by ads in magazines, or a combination of both methods. Even more fundamental, you will have to decide whether your test should be a "one-step" or a "two-step." These are not dance steps, but two different paths to making money in mail order.

The One-Step. If you run ads in magazines, or send direct-mail literature to prospects on a mailing lists, and *ask for an order directly*, then you are using the one-step method. There is only one step between you and an order, which can be cash, C. O. D., or a billing basis.

The Two-Step. If you run an ad, or send out literature, and invite the readers to *send for more information*, then you are using the two-step method. The first step is taken by the prospect when he responds to your offer of information. The second step occurs when you send the prospect the information he or she requested, and you ask for an order.

Both methods have been used successfully and there is no hard and fast rule that will tell you which one to use. However, there are certain guidelines that you will find helpful:

- The one-step method is generally more expensive in the beginning. In order to sell a product by mail, you have to describe it fully. This takes expensive space in a magazine or costly mail-order brochures in quantity. On the other hand, results are quick. As soon as the ad appears, the orders start coming in (provided the offer is a good one).
- The two-step is good for the beginner with limited capital. A small "teaser" ad in the classified columns of a

magazine can be quite inexpensive. On the other hand, after you've paid for the original inquiry, you still have to convert it into an order at additional expense. On the average, only about 10% to 20% of the people who respond to the ad for information will ultimately buy the product. This has to be allowed for in your cost calculations.

Use the one-step:

- When you want orders fast and your offer is not too expensive.
- When your profit margin is low and you can't afford a lot of follow-ups.
- When your budget permits taking larger space ads, or you can afford the mailing of many brochures to prospects on rented mailing lists.

Use the two-step:

- When you have to sift out prospects from a larger universe of possible buyers, or if you want to build a mailing list for other offers later on.
- When your product is fairly expensive and demands complete descriptions and illustrations.
- When your budget is limited and you want to find out quickly if there is any demand at all for the offer you have in mind.

Mail-order millions in magazines and mailing lists

You can reach your mail-order prospects by advertising in magazines that appeal to interest groups you want to reach or by renting appropriate mailing lists. Nowhere, we would guess, has more money been squandered than on poor decisions in these areas. Here we will give you some solid information that will help you to realize your $100-an-hour dream.

You have only to glance at any magazine stand to realize that there is a magazine for just about every interest group. Common sense also tells you that if you have a product or service for a special interest group, then you should seek a magazine that serves that area. This is not as easy to do as it may sound at first.

For example: if you're selling something for beekeepers, and there is only one magazine serving the interests of beekeepers, then your choice is obvious. But, what do you do if you're selling something of interest to handymen, and there are a dozen or so magazines appealing to this group. How do you pick the best one?

Go back to our original Power Shortcut: Find out what the other fellow is doing and copy his success. Examine various magazines in the area and read all the ads carefully. Answer these questions:

- Which ones carry the *most* ads for a product most like your own?
- Which publications cater to mail-order customers? Lots of ads *with coupons* mean that the magazine appeals to mail-order responsive people.
- Which magazine carries more classified ads? Page after page of such ads means that the magazine appeals to people who read and respond to small ads.

Finding the right publication in which to advertise

You have a product you want to sell by mail. You've browsed the local newsstand to see if there is a magazine or other publication in which it would make sense to advertise your product. You find no magazine serving the interest group you have in mind. What do you do?

You do what high-powered advertising agencies all over the country do in a similar situation. You do a little market research to seek out the best advertising media. Fortunately, the job is not at all difficult.

Two standard reference works are available in many libraries. If your local library doesn't carry them, your librarian can usually arrange for an inter-library loan from a library that does carry the reference works. The two references are the *Standard Rate and Data Service* and *Ayer's Guide to Periodical Literature*.

Standard Rate and Data Service is a monthly service that is published in several volumes covering *Consumer*, *Farm*, and *Business Magazines* and *Newspapers*. *Ayer's Guide* is an annual publication. Both are cross-referenced by subject areas so you can quickly see if there is a publication serving your needs. *Standard Rate and Data Service* is particularly useful if you have a product that serves the specialized needs of some industry, such as construction, food, retailing, automotive, etc.

Both publications give essential information regarding the circulation of the publication, frequency, size, cost of advertising, and other details. Before you decide on any one magazine, you should dig deeper for additional information not normally available in the reference books. Make a list of all the potential publications, including some marginal-interest ones, and then write to the business manager of each magazine and ask for a sample issue, a current advertising rate card, and any recent market studies made by the publication. The magazine will only be too happy to supply all this information to you if you mention that you are a potential advertiser. At the moment, there is no need to mention that you're only considering small space advertising.

When all this material arrives from a half dozen or more magazines, sit down and do some careful reading.

- Look over each publication and note whether ads such as the one you contemplate are carried.
- If two or more publications seem equal in this respect, then calculate the cost of reaching a single prospect. From the rate card, figure out what the same size ad in each of the publications would cost, then divide that by the circulation of the magazine to determine the cost of reaching a prospect. Obviously, other things being equal, the less it costs to reach a prospect with your message, the better the choice.
- Look at the market information each magazine supplies you. This is usually a tabulation of readership studies. These studies will tell you what kind of people read the magazine, where they live, their interests and hobbies, their annual income, and a host of other details about the readers who regularly get the magazine. A little common sense will tell you if these are the kinds of people who would be interested in your offer.

A mail-order pro's secret of picking a successful mailing list

In any company that does even a fair amount of business by mail, you will invariably discover a mailing-list pro—a specialist who spends all his time researching and selecting mailing lists to be used on various direct-mail campaigns. He usually commands a high salary and is worth it many times over.

No book could possibly give you the years of experience such a pro brings to his job. However, we will give you the basic principles he applies to every list decision so you, too, can have a high degree of successful direct-mail campaigns.

At the beginning of this chapter we mentioned the mail-order schemes you should avoid, particularly those that offer to supply you with "customer" names. If you knew the source of these names, what these customers bought, and how long ago they may have made such purchases, you would probably not waste any time even considering them. This brings up the following Power Shortcut:

Power Shortcut: Before you buy, rent, or use any mailing list, make sure you know the source and the age of the names.

The best way of assuring the accuracy of all this list information is to use the services of a reputable list broker. As a list user, you pay nothing to the broker; the list broker collects a commission from the list owner whose names you rent. Handling the paperwork of list rental is only a small part of a broker's job. He will research the market for you, make list recommendations, and within the limits of business ethics, he will also tell you what the experience of others has been in using a particular list.

If you don't know any reliable broker, you can get a current list of members from the Mailing List Brokers Professional Association, 663 Fifth Avenue, New York, NY 10022.

The "1 to 10 scale" of rating mailing lists

There are many subtle choices when you finally have to decide among a number of mailing lists that seem equally good. Over the years, we've developed a 1-to-10 scale of rating lists that will help you make a wise choice. A list rated 10 is absolutely the best; a list rated 6 is about average, while a list rated 1 or 2 is one you should avoid.

BEST–Scale of 10

The best list in the world is your own list of previous buyers. Unfortunately, the beginner in mail order has to accumulate a customer list over a period of time. However, once you've been in business for a while and have a list of customers, you have a gold mine. Not only can you sell these customers other products on a repeat basis, but you can also rent the names to non-competitors and make a handsome profit.

VERY GOOD–Scale of 8 to 9

Your own inquiry names rate next best. This is the reason why it is smart for a beginner to take small classified ads to generate inquiries, and then use direct mail to convert these inquiries into customers. In order to respond to a classified ad, a prospect has to find a postcard or some stationery, a postage stamp, and a pen or pencil. He has to write a message, often in his own handwriting, and then address the inquiry to a specific address. Then this inquiry has to be mailed. All this takes time and trouble, and the person who takes such pains to ask for additional information relating to your offer is a very hot prospect indeed!

GOOD–Scale of 6 to 7

Mail-order buyers of products similar to the one you are offering would fall in this class. Many of the lists a broker recommends will fall in this class, also. If you are selling a business book by mail and you can rent a mailing list of business book buyers, you could probably rate such a list as 7 on this scale. Buyers of business-related products, such as desk diaries, filing cabinets, and business stationery would rate a little lower—6 on this scale—as prospects for a business book.

FAIR to POOR–Scale of 4 to 5

Now you start entering the risky part of direct-mail selling. Most the lists we would include here are *not* demonstrated mail-order buyers. Here we would include members of associations or special-interest groups, subscribers to magazines, and lists compiled from directories or public records.

Many beginners in the mail-order business mistakenly think these lists are the most promising and waste a lot of time, effort, and money going after such prospects. The best prospects are those who have shown a willingness to *respond by mail*, either by ordering something or writing an inquiry letter. A person who is on a membership list of an organization is not necessarily a person who has an interest in doing business by mail. Approach all such lists with caution. Test them carefully.

VERY POOR—Scale of 1 to 3

Here we would include all "bargain" lists whose origin is unknown and any lists that are much over two years old. Here is where the advice of a good list broker is invaluable. If he's worth his commission, he knows the kinds of lists that would fall in this classification and will steer you clear of them.

This list classification system is very simple and you probably could memorize it if you took a moment or two to re-read the above pointers. It contains a great deal of valuable insider's know-how relating to the choice of mailing lists for direct-mail campaigns. We are constantly amazed at how much money is wasted by beginners because they do not know this simple guide to list selection. Now—how do you test a mailing list?

How to discover "hot" mailing lists with 3 simple testing techniques

To avoid expensive disappointments when you use a list there are three points to observe:

1) Use the previous checklist to rate the lists under consideration. Test the best best-rated lists first; if they don't work, you can be sure the lesser-rated lists will not be any better.

2) Get inside advice from a reputable broker for your particular offer. If he's any good, he'll know why certain lists might work better for you than some others.

3) Test . . . test . . . and test some more. This is the last and most important step in picking a list.

Testing is really very simple. You take a small sample of the whole list—usually around 2000 names—and mail your offer to the list. If the sample works, you test again with a larger group of names from the same list. This is called an extension mailing. If the extension works, you can go for the balance of the names on the list and pyramid your sales to dizzying heights.

A particular campaign might involve testing 10,000 names—2000 names from each of five different lists. How do you keep test results straight? Very simple. Your order card or form carries a code, either a letter or number, or some combination that makes sense to you. Each list you test is sent a card with a different code. As the orders come in, it is a simple matter to relate the specific order to a particular list.

Make up some simple record sheets, one sheet to a list. Record every result from that list on that sheet. Here are the things you should keep track of:

- The name and source of the list
- The number of names tested and the number of names remaining
- The number of orders
- The date of each order
- If your offer is a catalog of products, keep track of each item sold
- The reject or return rate. This is important. Sometimes you get an offer that works like wildfire, but a flood of returned merchandise will quickly kill your profits.

Taking the big step up to $100-an-hour income in mail order

Now we come to the important part of pyramiding your success upward to that magic income figure of $100 an hour. We've spent quite a few pages giving you the inside secrets discovering mail-order success items and how to go about testing your ideas at small cost. Once you start pyramiding, you enter the big leagues: big potential, big investments, big rewards.

Before you take a single step forward, you must recognize one important caution: A successful test is no guarantee that your pyramid will work as well as your tests. Sometimes your pyramid mailings work better; most of the time they seem to work a little less well than tests would suggest. Fortunately, you can make allowances for unknown factors and prevent a large loss of investment. Here's what to do:

- Pyramid your mailings upward with caution. Let's say the list you're testing has 100,000 names and that you tested 2000 names successfully. *Don't* under any circumstances, get carried away with dreams of instant wealth and invest everything you have in mailing to the balance of the list—98,000 names. Rather, mail to the list in steps, keeping accurate records as you go along.
- Depending on your knowledge and experience with a particular list (plus advice from a list broker), you should make extension mailings to a list at approximately a doubling rate. In other words: If 2000 names is your original test, your first extension should be around 5000 names, the next extension about 10,000 names, and so on. If the list is very unknown to you, test with extreme caution; if you've used it before and know what to expect, you can extend your mailings in bigger bites from the list.

- Always make sure you ask the list owner or the broker you're working with to eliminate all previously used names in your extension mailings. This will prevent you from going back to people who were in the segments of the list you originally tested. If a list owner can't do this for you, then you should be wary of the list. It probably means list maintenance is done very poorly, and there are a lot of old names and obsolete addresses in the list. Up-to-date lists are maintained on a computer, and it is easy for the computer to remember which names you used previously on a test.
- Recognize that all mail order is affected by the time of year in which you mail; some months are traditionally good mail-order months, while others are not. On a scale of 10, here is one such rating based on experience with millions of pieces mailed:

MONTH	RATING
January	10 (best)
February	9
March	7
April	7
May	7
June	6
July	7
August	8
September	8
October	9
November	8
December	8

- Use the table above until you develop one based on your own experience. It is handy for predicting results from your tests. For example: you can test a list in July and get 7 orders. If everything else remains the same, you should be able to get 10 orders from the same list and offer in January. Make your tests in poorer months; save the best months of the year for your big extension mailings.

If you've read the above carefully, you should now be aware of the fantastic potential available to you with proper pyramiding of results. Most important is the fact that you don't ever risk good money on something completely unknown or untried. Every investment you make is based on previously successful results.

The second fact is what makes $100 an hour possible in mail order; as you pyramid your results, you have a *cash flow*. Money is coming in each day. Each time you make an extension, you are using the money from a previous mailing. Assuming successful results from your tests, within a year you can easily be scheduling a mailing of 100,000 pieces. This, at current rates, would cost around $25,000 and should bring in about $75,000 in income.

Since your printer and your lettershop are doing all the manual work of putting a mailing out, your work is management only. Obviously, it takes the same amount of time on your part to schedule a mailing of 100,000 pieces as it does for 2000 pieces. The profit from such large mailings will easily exceed the $100 dollar-an-hour dream we are talking about.

Building repeat income in mail order

No businessman could stay in business for long if he depended exclusively on getting new customers. The secret of long-sustained success and growth in any business is to find a way to keep selling to your old and established customers. You have to do the same in mail order, too.

This means that the biggest, never-ending job in mail order is the search for new products to sell. However, once you've discovered one product that sells, it becomes much easier for you to find related items to sell to your customers.

Here's a good example: The publisher of the book you are now reading sells this book through mail-order efforts. In fact, you may have bought your copy as a result of a mail-order offer. By buying this book you have demonstrated to the publisher that you are ambitious and interested in making a big income. Therefore, you are undoubtedly also interested in books on advertising, building a small business, borrowing venture capital, and so on. The publisher will seek out such books, publish them, and make them known to you, building repeat business from valued customers. This brings up the next important Power Shortcut.

Power Shortcut: Once you have a mail-order success, search for related items of interest you can sell to your customers.

Fred G., whose story we told at the beginning of this chapter, discovered this Power Shortcut. If people are interested in birdhouses, he reasoned, they should be interested in bird baths, too. So he built a catalog of related items that eventually brought him success through repeat business.

Catalogs are a useful device for building repeat business and for testing mail order items. Once you have a half dozen items to sell, whether you put them on a single sheet of paper or actually print a booklet, you have a mail-order catalog.

Each time you mail the catalog, you code the order form to relate to the specific catalog you are mailing. Allocate the cost of the catalog among the various items that you are selling based on the amount of space they take up. If 10% of the space is taken up by one item, it should produce 10% of the income, other things being equal.

You will find that some items in a catalog will pay their way quite handsomely, while others may be disappointing. The next time you mail a catalog, remove the poor selling item and substitute another product. This way you build a catalog of best-selling items so that you are virtually assured of profit every time you mail it out.

Getting more income from each customer

Gillette, the man who invented the safety razor, was probably a better merchandising man than an inventor. He quickly realized that if his razor proved popular, he would make the most money on repeat purchases of blades over the years. Therefore, it made sense to give the razor away, or to make it low in cost to encourage people to buy.

You should seek the same thing in your mail-order business. Here are several ways of getting more dollars per customer:

- You can sell a product that uses consumable parts, such as in the safety razor example. If you sell bookkeeping supplies to accountants by mail, you will probably make more money over the years selling refills for the account books, rather than the books themselves.

- You can sell a relatively low-priced item at little or no profit in order to discover a customer for a higher-priced item. A well-known mail-order company sells auto-polishing cloths to car owners at a bargain price. The people who become customers are prime prospects for such big-ticket, high-profit items as custom auto slipcovers, floormats, custom accessories, and the like.

- You can develop a seasonal line of items that are good for automatic repeat business. Seed companies have discovered the value of this technique. When they get a customer, they know he will buy again and again as each year's catalog is sent to him.

You can probably think up some other ways of building repeat business and upgrading your customers to spend more with you. The important thing to remember is that you will never build a sustained, successful business if you concentrate on a one-time sale of one product.

Build your product line in related areas so that a customer of one item is a potential customer of another item in your line. Constantly test new products and don't be afraid to drop a loser *fast*. And finally, when you've gotten someone to buy from you, think up other ways of getting that customer to buy again and again *and again*.

The above pointers, some of which we have deliberately repeated because they are so important, represent the foundations for success in mail order. If you observe them, your chances of making up to $100 an hour are remarkably good; but it will take work and patience on your part.

However, all this information is useless unless you know how to apply it in a practical situation. You can learn all about engines, transmissions, clutches, and other auto theory, but to drive a car you still have to get experience on the road. In the next chapter, this is precisely what we intend to do. We will show you how to take all this foundation material on mail order and apply it, step by step, to many types of businesses.

9

tested "success secret" techniques that can make $100 an hour possible for you

In the previous chapter we discussed at length the fundamentals of successful mail-order businesses. Now we will take these fundamentals and translate them into step-by-step "success secret" techniques that you can use to build a business that has the potential of paying you $100 an hour for every hour you work.

Again, even if you decide to get into some business that is not primarily a mail order operation, you can apply many of these ideas to whatever you do.

Mail order, as you will recall, depends on good record keeping. Over the years, virtually every idea has been tested and a great deal of experience accumulated as to what works in mail order and what doesn't. Some of this information is readily available in books and magazine articles; other bits of information are jealously guarded secrets of successful mail-order operators. Here we will tell you the success secrets we have learned over the years with nothing held back.

Power Shortcut: The most valuable tool you can own in the mail-order business, or any business, is a sharp pencil.

We want to emphasize this fact because the biggest cause for grief and failure among beginners is their blind rush to get into the business without first doing some homework—mostly simple arithmetic. It is surprising how a little time spent in analyzing a project will often demonstrate that the "million-dollar-idea-that-can't fail" is really an impossible dream. On the other hand, what appears to be an ordinary idea or offer can often prove to have a surprising potential for profit.

Typically, a direct-mail campaign consists of a letter, a brochure, an order card or form, and the outgoing envelope to carry this material to some person on a mailing list.

If you performed the 100-postcard experiment we suggested in the previous chapter, you should have a lot of samples of mailing campaigns ranging all the way from cheap, mimeographed letters to lavish full-color brochures with personalized letters. Take some of these samples to various printers and ask for estimates. To get the true cost of mailing a similar campaign on your own offer, make sure you use the following checklist of costs:

Direct mail cost checklist

Printing

Include here all the estimates your printer gives you for printing the various pieces in a direct-mail campaign. This will include the letters, brochures, order forms, and envelopes. Remember that even your outgoing envelope will probably have a printed return address.

Circular handling

All your printed material will have to be collated, folded, and inserted in the outgoing envelope. The envelopes will have to be sealed, metered or stamped, and arranged in zip-code sequence if you intend to mail the pieces at the reduced rate for third-class bulk mail. For your first mailing of a thousand or two, you and your family will probably do this job with gusto. After that, you should get estimates for this work from a lettershop. Your printer can recommend one.

Postage

Postage rates have changed so often we won't even mention a figure here because it is bound to be out of date. Rather, go to your local post office and talk to the postmaster. You can save big money by getting a bulk-mail permit, but certain mailing rules have to be observed.

List rental

If you are generating prospect names through your own space ads, your records will tell you how much each prospect's name is costing you. If you rent a mailing list through a list broker (more about this later), you will be charged for the names for a one-time rental. You will have to pay for a minimum number of names—2000 to 5000 names—and also pay the cost of putting these names on your envelope. The lettershop has equipment to take sheets of names, cut them up into individual labels, and glue them on your envelopes. These are called Cheshire labels or tapes.

Add costs carefully

When you get all these costs, ask the printer and lettershop for estimates on various quantities. If you mail a small test quantity, the costs will be relatively high; larger mailings will be much cheaper. A good selection of quantities for getting estimates is as follows:

- 2000 pieces—for the initial test
- 10,000 pieces—for extensions of test mailings
- 50,000 pieces—for mailings to large lists that have been tested successfully

When you get your estimate of costs, make sure you include important one-time costs, also. You might have to pay for photography or artwork illustrating your product, special type for printing the brochures, engravings, and the like.

When you have added up all these costs, divide it by the *number of thousands* of pieces you plan to mail to get your *cost per thousand pieces mailed.* If you figure everything at so much per thousand pieces, this part of the estimate will be easy. Immediately, you have some valuable information.

For example: Let's assume you want to sell a $5 item through the mail. Your estimate of costs for a direct-mail campaign might come to $250 per thousand pieces mailed. In order to recover *just the cost of the mailing,* you would have to get 50 orders per thousand pieces mailed ($250 ÷ $5 = 50 orders). Of course you also have to sell a substantial additional quantity to recover the cost of your product, too. Depending on how much your product costs, you might have to get 60 or 70 orders just to break even.

How much should you expect?

If you're new to the mail-order business, you might think that 70 orders per thousand pieces mailed is a fairly reasonable expectation. Experience will prove otherwise; if you get 20 to 30 orders per thousand, you're doing quite well. If you depend on more than this in your estimating, you're bound to lose money.

Your sharp pencil has just saved you hundreds of dollars: Now use your pencil to see what is needed to make you break-even. You can:

- Reduce the cost of your mailing piece by using cheaper paper, less color, or some other printing economy.
- Increase printing quantities for a price break (assuming, of course, that your tests say "go").

- Get your product costs down.
- Increase your retail selling price.
- Make your order handling more economical.
- Change your offer to eliminate expensive "fringes." Ask the customer to add additional money for postage and handling; insist on payment with order to eliminate billing expenses, etc.

Without knowing what specific offer you have in mind, it is impossible for us to give you a precise example of the savings possible. However, from this list, it should be apparent to you that mail-order selling is basically an exercise in fascinating arithmetic. It is amazing how this attention to detail can pay off. If you get your costs down a fraction, get your price up a fraction, and increase customer response to your mailing another fraction, you can often turn a lackluster mailing into a solid profit maker—one that can put you on the road to $100 an hour.

How to make a test mailing pay off

You're anxious to start; your pencil says "go" and you want to know what to do next. You might want to review our suggestions on rating mailing lists that we mentioned in Chapter 8. Testing the best list first is good business sense. If the best list doesn't work, the poorer ones certainly won't. If it does work, the test results will give you a cash flow that you can quickly pyramid upward with additional mailings.

How many lists should you test?

The answer will be determined by several things, the first and most important being the amount of money you have to invest. If your initial investment is small—say a few hundred dollars at most—then you will be limited to testing perhaps one good list. Be patient. Test the list and await results. If it works, the cash flow generated will enable you to test a couple of more lists the next time around. Again, this is the pyramid of results working for you.

If you have your choice of several lists that appear equally good, and assuming that your budget can stand the expense, then test several lists.

How many names should you test on a list?

There is a lot of misunderstanding on this point. Many experienced mail-order people still think that you have to test a certain percentage of a list in order to be sure of results. For example, they will test 1000 names from a list of 10,000 prospects; 5000 names from a 50,000 list, or some similar constant like 5% or 10% of the total names.

Nothing could be further from the truth.

Regardless of the size of a mailing list in total, you can get very valid test results from a relatively small sample *if* that sample is truly representative of the entire list. Getting an absolutely perfect sample of the entire list is impossible, so the problem of picking a sample size is somewhat more complicated.

The size of your test mailing should be big enough to generate at least 25 orders. If you get much less than 25 orders from a list, it is risky to assume you will get the same percentage of orders on a larger sample or the whole list.

If you get very few orders from a list and try to extend these results, you might misjudge the real acceptance of your offer. One or two orders more or less affect the percentage of responses greatly when total orders number only a dozen or so. On the other hand, two or three orders more or less in a total response of 25 to 30 orders causes much less uncertainty.

Getting help from experts

How do you know how many names to test in order to generate 25 to 30 orders? This is where experience with your product and the mailing list come into play. There is no other way to answer this question. After a while, you will get the idea of how your orders are running and how many names you should test whenever you're testing a list. In the beginning, look for advice from your list broker. He is experienced with the lists he is recommending and should probably have some idea of results achieved by others with a similar offer.

Generally speaking, the lower the price, the more orders you can expect. As price goes up, the response goes down percentage-wise, but your *dollar income can still be rising*. Remember, you put dollars in your bank account, not percentages. Therefore, don't assume that there is some magic percentage response you should shoot for—like 2% or 3% or what have you. Always look for total dollars that pay all your expenses and still leave you a profit.

Before you think of mailing your first campaign, there is another important matter that should be attended to, and it leads to an important Power Shortcut.

Power Shortcut: Uncle Sam wants to help you in every way possible to make your dream of $100 an hour come true. Meet him at your local post office.

When you decide to go into the mail-order business, you immediately acquire a partner—the United States Postal Service. They deliver your mail to prospects out there ... they deliver orders back to you ... and then they deliver the goods to your customers. They even help you collect the money. This is a mighty important partner to take into your business, yet it is amazing how many beginners in mail order do not even take the trouble to meet their postmaster.

The author knows two people, Joe and Edith T., who started a mail-order business selling specialized music records to elementary school teachers. The product was so needed by teachers that Joe and Edith made a nice profit in spite of several elementary mistakes. For example: At first they sent all their mail via expensive first class. Joe and Edith didn't even know that a lower third-class business rate existed until their postmaster advised them to change to that rate.

This simple change added thousands of dollars to their profit line the first year!

Meet your postmaster. Introduce yourself to "the boss" at the office where you'll be doing business, and explain your business. You'll be pleasantly surprised at the help the postmaster can give you. While he can't bend the postal laws for you or anyone else, he can show you how to expedite your mail, ensure prompt delivery, and save postage costs when you mail.

Rent a post office box early in your plans. If you know your postmaster well, he can tell you which box numbers are empty and available, or will soon be available. It's a good idea to get a box number which will be easy for customers to remember—like Box 10 or Box 100. This is especially important if you ever want to try your hand at radio advertising; it will make your spoken address easier to recall by people who don't have a pencil and paper handy.

Also, tell your postmaster *all* the names you expect customers to use in sending you mail. List your personal and business names and even the names of your products. You will be surprised at the various names customers can dream up when they are writing you a letter. If your postmaster knows you and what you're doing, it will help get more mail delivered to you and less returned to sender with the notation "addressee unknown."

Here are additional things "your partner" will help you with:

- *Bulk mail permits.* To get the lower third-class business rate, you will have to get a permit to mail at lower bulk mail rates. Often a lettershop will do this service for you at the post office they use. However, our feeling is that you're much better off dealing with your local postmaster. For example, when you have a big mailing coming up, alert your "friend at the post office" and he will be able to plan for your added workload, and will appreciate it.

- *Business reply mail.* If you want people to send orders to you, you must make it easy for them to do so. One of the best ways is by use of the business reply card or envelope. You've seen these often, with printed bars running down one side and the words, "Postage will be paid by such and such company." Many people are under the mistaken impression that the postage must be paid on each printed card sent out, which could be a terrific expense. Actually, the workings of this mail-order device are quite simple and inexpensive:

  1) You get a permit for business reply mail from your post office.

  2) The postmaster assigns you a number which is printed on your envelopes up in the corner where a stamp usually goes. You pay only for the permit, not for subsequent printings of this "indicia" as it is called.

  3) When the mail is returned to you with orders, it is treated like a C. O. D. mailing—you pay the postage due plus a surcharge for the service. This is a small expense to pay for an order, especially when

the cumulative experience of hundreds of mailers prove that business-reply mail increases response from a mailing.
- *Postage stamps.* Often you will want to use a stamp on your outgoing envelope instead of the postage imprint of a meter. Pre-cancelled stamps are available for mailing at bulk rates. If you are mailing something first class, then stamps can be obtained in rolls which fit inexpensive stamp-affixing machines. These are handy for correspondence, also. Again, your friendly postmaster can tell you when a particularly appropriate commemorative stamp is coming in case you want to use this technique to attract more attention to your letters.
- *Other services.* The post office provides a supermarket of services to businessmen. Parcel post, registration, certified, and priority mail are only a few of the services. By working closely with your postmaster, you will discover cost-cutting techniques of mailing and delivering packages that can increase your "bottom line" to the magic point where you're making that $100 an hour.

Important first impressions

No one needs to tell you how all-important first impressions can be—especially if you're a salesman making a call for the first time on a potential customer. This first impression is equally important when you're in the mail-order business, and the first impression you make is with your envelope.

You wouldn't think of calling on a customer without paying careful attention to every item of your attire; yet, many mailers ignore this principle and buy any old envelope kicking around the print shop when they place an order.

Power Shortcut: You will never make a sale if your prospect doesn't open your envelope. Therefore, do everything possible to make your envelope stand out from the rest of the mail, and invite attention inside.

When you stop to think about the matter for a moment, this Power Shortcut seems so obvious that it shouldn't even rate a mention. Yet, look at the mail you receive the next few days and pick out those envelopes that truly attract your attention and say "open me first!"

You'll probably be amazed at how hum-drum most of the envelopes in your pile of mail are. Therefore, the first thing to do is to use every means possible to take your letter out of the "ordinary" and into the "extraordinary" pile. Here are some ways to do that job, based on the experience of mail-order masters.

Size

The size of the envelope suggests what's inside. The ordinary #6 envelope (which is 6½ inches long) is typically used for personal letters. If you want your message to appear personal, especially if you're typing the address instead of using labels, then this size might be very effective. Remember, however, that you won't be able to cram a very large letter or brochure inside.

The regular # 10 envelope (which is 9½ inches long) is the standard-size envelope used in the majority of business correspondence. Because this size is so common, it is hard to make it stand out unless you adopt a few ideas we will mention in a moment below.

The baronial envelope (which is about 4½ by 5½ inches) is more like a square and usually suggests important invitations. If you're inviting prospects to join a club of some sort or to become subscribers to some publication or project, this could be the very envelope to use.

Another device available in different sizes of envelopes is the glassine window. This serves a double purpose: envelopes like this are traditionally used for bills and important documents, so the tendency on the part of the recipient is to treat it with care and to note the contents carefully.

This type of envelope is also useful if you're using mailing lists on labels. Instead of pasting them on a solid envelope, the label can be pasted on an order form which shows through the window. That way, when you get the order back, you can be sure of reading the name and address easily, and it also makes it a trifle easier for the customer to order if he doesn't have to write out his full name and address.

Again, please check with your postmaster before using any non-standard envelope. Increasingly, the automated machinery in the post office will reject such envelopes, and you will be able to mail them only by paying a premium over regular postage.

Color

Most envelopes are white, so a colored envelope will automatically stand out in a pile. Keep these cautions in mind, however: dark envelopes, while very dramatic, are difficult to address unless you use a label. The white label then destroys the overall effect by making it look like a patch. Dark colors are usually more expensive than white or very light colors, so you have to consider the expense of increased attention value relative to the extra business the color might or might not bring you.

Message

A useful and time-honored way to get your reader interested in your offer is to start it right on the envelope. This is called a "teaser" for obvious reasons. The few words tease the reader into wanting to know more about what is inside and he proceeds to open the envelope. Great ideas for teasers invariably provoke curiosity, promise something new or free, or otherwise offer some reward for opening the envelope.

How to write copy that sells

Now that your envelope is opened, you've got to make good on that promise to the reader. In other words, your letter, brochure, or other message must attract the reader from start to finish. You have to sell your idea, product, or service, to the readers and you do it with words. The words are called "copy" and the person who writes them is a "copywriter."

Skilled copywriters have been known to make six-figure incomes because their skill is so important in selling, and it can mean millions of dollars worth of business to a client. Volumes have been written on the subject, and courses abound. Yet when all is said and done, the whole secret of successful copywriting can be summed up in the following Power Shortcut.

Power Shortcut: Hey! You! See? So!

This Power Shortcut was suggested by a well-known teacher and writer some years ago in a book.* Although he didn't call it a Power Shortcut, it certainly does qualify as one because these four words sum up everything that should appear in an effective sales message.

How to use this four-part formula to sell more

Hey!

In the beginning you've got to attract the attention of your reader in some fashion. You don't really yell *Hey!* but the effect is the same. On the envelope and in the headline of

---

Writing Non-Fiction, Walter S. Campbell, The Writer, Inc., Boston, 1944.

your message, you have to make some statement to attract attention and make the reader want to know more. Usually this statement is a promise of some benefit that will appeal to the reader, like saving time or money, gaining success, or preventing something undesirable from happening. Your product suggests the major benefits you should stress.

You!

Here is where most inexperienced copywriters make a mistake. They like to write about their company, their business, their reputation and the like. As soon as you attract your reader's attention with some benefit you should look at it from the reader's point of view. In other words, everything should be *you . . . you . . . you!* Your reader is not much interested in what you say about yourself, but he is interested in *himself*. Show him how your product or service will benefit *him* specifically.

See?

Now come the explanations. Your reader will want to see clearly how your product will help him, how to use it, who recommends it, why it is a bargain, and a host of other details before he makes up his mind to buy. List all these thoughts in order of importance and describe them clearly and simply in the sales message. These are the reasons why he should buy, and they should be numerous, interesting, and convincing.

So!

This is the clincher where you ask for an order. Surprisingly enough, many otherwise good salesmen fall down on this score whether they are selling in person or in a printed message. In fact, Richard P. Ettinger, who was the president of a large publishing company, constantly reiterated this fact by saying, "The worst sin a salesman can commit is *not* to ask for the order!" So, always ask for the order. Tell the reader why he should order now. Make it easy to order, and don't forget to tell him your guarantees of satisfaction and returns policy.

This four-part formula digests everything you need to know about writing hard-selling copy in mail order and every other type of media. If you've done the 100-postcard experiment that we suggested in the previous chapter, you should have a lot of samples to examine and study for copywriting hints. As another experiment, sort out those samples that appeal to you for one reason or another. Apply the four-part, *hey!, you!, see?, so!* formula and the chances are very good that each and every piece satisfies this formula in some ingenious way.

Other secrets of mail-order success

Mail-order isn't limited to direct-mail pieces sent out to prospects on a list. Here are a few of the other ways insiders in this business make money apart from mailings:

- *Space advertising.* Any advertisement you see in a magazine with a coupon is a mail-order advertisement. These are particularly numerous in specialized magazines that serve some interest group like car enthusiasts, photography buffs, stamp collectors, and the like.
- *Radio and television advertising.* Most of the ads you hear and see are straight commercials for some consumer product. However, local stations often carry offers selling books, records, kitchen appliances, and other merchandise. The commercial ends with a repetition of order instructions such as, "Send $5.95 to Smash Hits, in care of . . ."
- *Matchbooks.* Look at the matches you have in your pocket right now. This is a favorite medium for corre-

spondence schools, courses, and other products and services that appeal across a broad range of people. Usually a coupon is printed on the inside cover.
- *Co-op mailings.* A mailer will often plan a large mailing to a specific target group of prospects. In order to cut down costs, he offers to sell space in his mailings to non-competing products. The mailer benefits because he is able to share heavy expenses with outside people. The outsiders sharing the same envelope benefit because they only pay a small share of the total cost of reaching the market.

The above list covers some important mail-order selling mediums, but is by no means a complete list. Some others would include handouts of one sort or another, inserts in packages and newspapers, catalog agencies, party plans, and others.

In your study of mail-order techniques, always keep that four-part, *hey!*, *you!*, *see?*, *so!* formula in mind. Whether the offer is conveyed in large and elaborate full-color brochure or on the back of a lowly matchbook cover, the ads that get attention and sell invariably follow this formula.

Mail order success on a shoestring

Over the years, smart mail-order operators have discovered a number of ways of making it big on a shoestring. A large mailing to several dozen lists is exciting to plan, but expensive to produce. If you mailed 100,000 pieces (which is moderate in mail-order terms) the cost would be at least $20,000 and possibly as high as $30,000. In the beginning it's unlikely that you would be in a position for such a gamble—and we wouldn't recommend it even if you had the money.

However, there are ways of reducing your investment and risk down to an acceptable minimum. Our next Power Shortcut explains how.

Power Shortcut: Get others to help you share the risk by offering them a share of the profits.

We can best demonstrate the workings of the Power Shortcut by telling you the story of Warren B. that we mentioned at the beginning of the book. As you recall, Warren B. was a clerk in the personnel department of a large company. He had security, but a modest salary and not much chance to make it big in his own company.

In addition, Warren had access to personnel records and in the course of his work discovered the salaries and fringe benefits that the executives in his company enjoyed. When Warren looked at their huge five-figure incomes, their expense accounts, company cars, and paid-up dues to the best clubs, he was determined that he would enjoy the same rewards somehow.

This Power Shortcut made it possible for him to live as well as the top executives in his company—and then some! He was also his own boss. Here's the step-by-step reasoning that Warren applied and which you can use as a model for your own thinking.

1) Warren saw hundreds of people hired through his work in the personnel department, but all these people were at the low and middle job ranges—clerks, typists, factory help, supervisors, and the like. Where do executives come from? How are the top jobs filled?

2) Warren asked some questions of his supervisor, and started reading personnel magazines in earnest. Soon he discovered his answer: top executives are usually recruited by executive search specialists of one sort or another.

3) Warren never saw a top executive enter his personnel department looking for a job, so it was obvious that they worked through these specialists. Who were

these specialists? Where were they located? Again Warren had to do a little digging, mostly at his local library.

4) Warren discovered that no single list existed of all the various executive search agencies, management consultants, and specialists in this area. Then *the idea* struck him. Top executives looking for a change in jobs would probably pay handsomely for such a list. An executive could prepare a resumé of his background, make copies, and then send this information to selected names on the list. Among all these specialists actively searching for executives for a variety of top clients, it was quite likely that a number of profitable job interviews could result.

5) Warren set about preparing just such a list. Actually, it turned out to be a fairly large directory of names compiled from telephone books all across the country, professional rosters, and the membership lists of professional societies that these executive specialists belonged to.

Warren now had a "classic" mail-order product to sell. Recall some of the things we mentioned when we spoke about choosing a mail-order product in the previous chapter and how Warren met them:

- Warren's directory was unique. The complete list of names he developed was not conveniently available in any one source.
- Warren had information to sell. It's much easier to get a high price for information than it is for physical merchandise where people can readily set some value.
- Warren controlled his inventory. He could print as many or as few copies of his directory as he wished. If business turned out great, he could quickly reprint

copies and avoid customer disappointments because of out-of-stock situations.
- The product was easy to ship and damage-proof in ordinary mail.

Now two big questions remained, and the answer to both required money—and Warren had only a very limited amount to invest in this idea. He needed money to print the book and money to sell the book. This Power Shortcut solved both these problems because it helped him get others interested in the idea of sharing the risk.

Making deals with a printer

Printers are human like anyone else and will often be intrigued by an idea sufficiently to want to invest in it. However, printers usually have another compelling reason to be on the lookout for such deals. Printing presses represent a big capital investment, and like all investments in machinery, they must be kept busy to make a profit.

If a printer has "downtime"—a period when the press is not running—it will still cost him money in overhead expenses of the shop, interest on the loan that paid for the press, warehousing costs on paper supplies, and the like. Warren simply hunted around until he found a printer with a downtime situation on his hands and made a deal.

"Look," said Warren to the printer, "if you let the downtime add up you know for sure that it will cost you plenty with no chance of recovering any money for lost hours. But, if you take a chance with me on my idea, I promise to repay you out of any profits. No guarantee, but even a slim chance is better than no chance!"

This kind of talk made sense to the printer and they struck a deal with a bit of compromise. Warren would have a typist prepare a neatly-typed manuscript that could be used by the printer instead of setting expensive type for the directory. In addition, Warren agreed to share the actual cost of the paper used on the small first run.

Soon Warren had the pleasure of seeing his first mail-order product roll off the press. Now the next problem was to sell it. If the Power Shortcut worked with the printer, why couldn't it work someplace else?

Making deals with magazines for free advertising

Every magazine has so many pages to fill each month, yet you will never see a blank page or even a few inches of column space that is blank. How come? The secret is "filler space." Every publication has material on hand that it will use in desperation to make the pages come out even. Often this material is a free plug for some charity or a patriotic message.

The situation is similar to the downtime experience of the printer. By running filler space, the publisher of the magazine knows that he will get nothing in return, other than a neat-looking page. Notwithstanding the expense of the space in the magazine, a publisher will listen to any deal which holds out a promise to pay him *something* for space that would otherwise earn nothing in advertising revenues.

Warren used the same arguments with a number of publishers that he used with his printer friend. Only this time Warren had a lot more people to contact, and he did it this way:

1) Warren went to the library again and compiled a list of all the magazines that served the interests of higher-level managers and executives. Many of these publications (which were listed by category in *Standard Rate and Data*) appealed to specific industry or occupational groups.

2) After eliminating the really big magazines serving executives, such as *Business Week*, *Forbes*, *Fortune* and some others, Warren had a list of several hundred medium and smaller specialized publications to solicit with his offer to share the profits of his directory.

Warren wrote the following letter to each publisher (whose name he got in the same *Standard Rate and Data*).

Dear

Recently my company published the *Directory of Executive Recruitment Specialists,* and I think your publication would be a good magazine in which to advertise this book. However, there are many other magazines to choose from and my advertising budget will not permit testing each one.

I would like to suggest the following offer which, if successful, should make us both a lot of money. My company will prepare an advertisement in any size you suggest that would be used by you whenever filler space is available in your publication.

This will be a tasteful ad that will be run over your name as the selected distributor of this directory. All orders and money would come to you directly. Simply forward the orders to us and we will drop ship the directory within 24 hours to your customers. We will pay you a 40% commission on every sale you make.

Both of us know that filler space earns you nothing. Even if the income from this commission ad is less than what you would ordinarily earn selling advertising space at your regular rates, it is a positive contribution to profits on your bottom line.

If this suggestion makes good business sense to you, please let me know and I will immediately send you a copy of the directory to examine first hand and get to work preparing an advertisement for your magazine.

Sincerely,

Warren B.

A simple, forthright letter like this impressed a lot of the publishers receiving it. Smaller publishers usually have the most trouble filling space, so they respond in more numbers. Soon, orders started rolling in, too.

Warren didn't make his fortune from this one publication or sales effort. But this Power Shortcut got him going on the track toward a big income and independence in a business of his own. As the money rolled in, Warren began to accumulate capital for more ambitious projects.

Think for a few minutes how you could duplicate Warren's success. With the right product you could:

- Approach publishers of magazines in areas other than those selected by Warren.
- Offer the same commission deal to radio and TV stations. They have "filler" time available and are just as anxious to get good commission deals. (Don't waste your time with large network stations; stick with small local stations, especially FM stations.)
- Work a similar arrangement with a small local newspaper.
- At the very least, interest a suitable retail outlet to handle your product on a commission basis.

The principle of this Power Shortcut seems to work best in the mail-order field and is the reason why we discussed it at length in this chapter. However, as you will see in later chapters there are ways of combining this Power Shortcut with others to advance you on the road to the $100-an-hour goal you have set for yourself.

10

how to earn up to $100 an hour while working for someone else

One of the first questions that always comes up when we discuss the idea of making $100 an hour with friends is this:

"How can you ever get to the point of making $100 an hour in some activity if you're tied down with a job? Making this kind of money takes time, and few people can gamble their life savings by quitting their job and striking out in some new business."

Our answer is always the same, "Don't even think of quitting your job until you are making up to $100 an hour every hour you care to work, and you are absolutely sure you can repeat that performance day in and day out."

A pretty big order, but you will see on the following pages some examples of people who have done just that—made fortunes on their own while working for someone else. Often these people continue working at their jobs because they enjoy the variety it brings to their day, or they meet interesting people with stimulating ideas.

How to work your way up to $100 an hour

We would not be honest with our readers if we promised them some magic formula that would earn them $100 an hour the first time they tried it. Nobody can do that. What we will be doing constantly is showing you tested ways of working toward that goal.

If you make $5 or $10 an hour the first few times you try something on your own, you've taken the first step toward $100 an hour. How long it takes you to get there will depend on how hard you want to work toward that goal.

We will try to make that journey as easy as possible by giving you what we feel are the shortcuts—we call them Power Shortcuts. In order to earn $100 an hour while still holding down a regular job, you should keep this Power Shortcut constantly in mind:

Power Shortcut: Use your present job as a foundation on which to build a $100-an-hour income figure.

In your quest for wealth, it is often easy to forget how important your current job can be in making your dreams come true. This is true even if by some chance you feel your job is humdrum and lacking in any excitement or future. Let's look at your present job and see why it is so important in your overall plan for independence.

1) Security is the first thought that comes to mind. Think of a businessman who is trying to make a go of it in a business that he started with borrowed money. He has to worry about making money on a day-to-day basis to pay his bills. He has that big loan on his mind constantly. And, if the business should fail, how would he provide for himself and his family?

2) Fewer worries are an important second point to keep in mind. Our businessman is never free from worry,

how to earn up to $100 an hour while working for someone else 197

and it is certain that his concerns sometime keep him from making the best business decisions—especially if they entail some element of risk. With a permanent job that puts bread on the table and a roof over your head, you can treat your beginning efforts at wealth building almost as a hobby, and also try many things to discover which works best for you.

3) Your current job can be a very important source of ideas that can help you reach your goal of $100 an hour. Even a boring factory production-line job can have rewards in this area. Think about ways to improve some machine or process you work with. Can you patent the idea and sell it to a big company, or possibly even to your own company? If you work in an office, think about the people you meet each day both in your company and outside your company. Do they share ideas with you? Can they be a source of contacts?

The point is abundantly clear—don't sacrifice your job until you have your money machine working smoothly. And, once you've got your money machine ticking smoothly, you might even want to tinker with it to make it produce income on a big scale—like $100 an hour. This is just what Tom H. did.

You may recall from the introduction to this book that we briefly mentioned how Tom achieved a part-time income of $180 a week. People said he was crazy because he applied the following Power Shortcut and saw his income drop to $40 a week! But . . . read on and see the real wisdom behind Tom's action.

Power Shortcut: Once you have something working making money, bring in helpers—even if it causes a temporary drop in your income.

Tom worked the four o'clock to midnight shift in a food processing plant, which meant he had free time in the morning and early afternoon to experiment with part-time businesses. He tried several until he achieved a fair degree of success with a cleaning service business. It was hard work and really meant that he was holding down two jobs.

When his cleaning business was averaging about $180 a week (which was about what he was earning at the plant) his wife and friends urged him to quit his job and go into the cleaning business full-time. Tom analyzed his situation and came up with these pros and cons:

- PRO: By quitting his job at the plant he would finally be independent in a business of his own.
- CON: His business wasn't that well established, so quitting his job would mean gambling with his security.
- PRO: If he worked hard, he could make the business grow.
- CON: In order to make his business grow, he would have to hire a helper, and the business wouldn't fully support two people.
- PRO: The business seemed assured of success because there was no competition in the area.
- CON: But that was no guarantee that someone with more capital couldn't open a competing business and wipe him out.

Tom solved this dilemma by applying the Power Shortcut we mentioned. He did the following:

1) He kept his job at the plant. This eliminated day-to-day worries of paying his bills and providing for his family.
2) He hired a helper to work in the business. Hiring the helper immediately meant meeting a weekly wage for

an employee and additional taxes for unemployment insurance, social security, and the like. But, even more important, after paying all these expenses Tom had $40 a week left over as pure profit from the work of his employee. In other words, Tom could earn $40 a week free and clear from this business without lifting a finger. His helper earned the money for him. The dazzling possibility in this situation became crystal clear when Tom planned the growth of his business on paper. It looked like this:

TOM'S PROFIT PLAN

Number of People Working	Income	Wages	Profit to me
Myself (I do all the work)	$ 180	$ 0	$180
1 Helper (He does all the work))	$ 180	$140	$ 40
2 Helpers (They do all the work)	$ 360	$280	$ 80
3 Helpers (They do all the work)	$ 540	$420	$120
4 Helpers (They do all the work)	$ 720	$560	$160
5 Helpers (They do all the work)	$ 900	$700	$200
6 Helpers (They do all the work)	$1080	$840	$240

If Tom added his own work in the cleaning business to the above totals, his weekly income could jump to $420 a week after he had added 6 helpers. And he would still be earning money at the plant on a regular, week-in and week-out basis.

Needless to say, Tom's future did not work out with the precision of the arithmetic shown above. The cleaning business depends on people to do the work and there is a pretty close relationship between the number of people you employ and the amount of business you can handle.

However, by the time he had hired his fourth helper, the money coming in enabled Tom to add more efficient cleaning equipment and to take on bigger and more expensive jobs. He graduated into industrial and commercial cleaning where he got business on a guaranteed contract basis. In addition, he bid on cleaning some municipal buildings and was awarded a city contract.

Tom was able to quit his plant job by this time secure in the knowledge that his business was growing, providing security for his family, and earning more money than he could ever have dreamed of earning working for someone else.

Yet, if Tom had quit his plant job prematurely, he would have struggled in all likelihood in a small cleaning business, never able to hire the helpers he needed to make his business grow. In the beginning, these helpers cost money, but in the end they provided Tom with an income that had the potential of $100 an hour. All this was possible because Tom used Power Shortcuts; he used his job as a foundation on which to build a business, and he wisely brought in helpers at the beginning.

How to find time to make $100 an hour while working for someone else

"I don't have a job like Tom's which leaves my mornings and afternoons free. How can I find the time to work toward $100 an hour?" This is a question that many are asking at this moment and here is our answer.

Wasted hours can be wealth hours

Get a piece of paper and chart a typical day in your life. Put down the actual hours you are committed to spend on your job, on necessary household chores, and in outside activities. Then add time for eating, sleeping, and recreation. You'll surprise yourself with the number of "wasted" hours in your "typical" day.

How are these hours wasted? Idly watching TV when no special program interests you. Loafing around the house.

Stretching out the time it takes to do errands or chores. You could name a hundred different ways time is wasted.

Checklist of wealth hours available to you

In talking with people and showing them how to organize their time around a wealth-building activity, we have discovered many idle hours that can be turned into profitable chunks of time. Here are some of them:

- *In the early morning.* The author of this book is an early riser out of habit. Most of this book was written during the cool, quiet hour or so before the rest of the family gets up for breakfast.
- *Going to work.* If you have to spend time commuting on a bus or railroad train, count yourself lucky. This enforced hour or two of "captivity" can be put to good use planning details of your business, answering letters, or doing paperwork.
- *During lunchtime.* A lot of people use their lunch hours to advantage. You can deal with suppliers, make business calls, sell things, or close big deals with business contacts in a posh restaurant.
- *Returning home from work.* Do some of the same things you did in the morning. Also, this is a good time to plan what you will do in the evening so you can accomplish much without wasting a lot of time thinking about what you're going to do.
- *Waiting for supper to be ready.* A great time to catch up on your mail or to write checks. Tedious chores like this are always handled best in such odd moments because they seem to get done without cutting into other profitable hours.
- *In the evening.* Do you really want to watch that old re-run on TV? Even if your beginning wealth activities

are netting you only $5 an hour, wasting an hour in front of the TV really means you "spent" $5 to watch that old show. Put a value on your time and you won't waste it.
- *On weekends.* Most people live for the weekends when they can get away from the job. What better way is there to "get away" from a dull job than to work on your own plans for independence earning up to $100 an hour every hour you work.
- *On vacations.* Again, vacations should take you away from the job for a change of scene and recreation. By all means, have a good time. But keep your eyes and mind alert to opportunities in different locations. Is there a supplier of an item that could be a good mail-order product located nearby? Did you meet some people who could become customers, partners, or just idea stimulators? Is this new place you're visiting a possible site for a business activity with more potential than you have in your home town? Ask yourself lots of questions like this.
- *An enforced period of idleness.* Think of all the times you waste waiting for something to happen. In doctor's offices. In airplane terminals. Even hospital beds can be turned into "offices" if you're confined with something like a broken leg which doesn't drain your energies. Consider how many best sellers have been written in prison.

Set up a plan for regular work

All these ideas depend on one preliminary detail. The best way of impressing on you the importance of this step is to describe it as a Power Shortcut.

Power Shortcut: Be ready always to turn odd hours into "golden hours."

Your grandmother probably used this Power Shortcut. She would keep a basket of mending and mending supplies nearby in the kitchen. While waiting for the potatoes to boil, a sock could be darned.

We know an author who always carries a small writing case as he travels to his city office on the train to and from his home in a luxury suburb. Other commuters grumble about delays, argue about sports or politics, or simply disappear into the bar car. He turns out two pages a day, one in the morning and one in the evening as he travels to and from work.

Two pages a day comes to ten pages a week. In a relatively few months time he has written another book. Over the years, his books have earned him humdreds of thousands of dollars—rather nice hourly pay for normally "wasted" hours.

Few of us have the talent to turn out top-selling books year in and year out. But all of us can put such hours to profitable use in other ways. All it takes is preparation, usually of the simplest kind. Use this checklist to help your thinking on using these hours:

- Always have pencil and paper as part of your "kit." It is amazing how many good ideas can be stimulated if you get into the habit of writing out your thoughts and plans.
- Have necessary stationery supplies to carry you through an hour or two. If you're going to use these hours to answer your mail, make sure you take some pre-stamped envelopes so you can complete the job.
- A small reference notebook is another part of your kit. In this notebook list important names and phone numbers, prices of services or supplies you use in your business, and a calendar to help in your planning.
- You might also want to carry a brief outline of your business income and expenses. By taking a few min-

utes to study these figures at odd moments, you can often discover some aspect of your business that can be changed or improved to increase your hourly return. And remember—every step upward puts you that much closer to your goal of making $100 an hour.

How to discover profitable ideas while working for someone else

"I can't write books. I'm not a financial wizard. I'm just plain stumped when it comes to thinking up ideas that could earn me up to $100 an hour. What do I do?" We've heard all these comments from people who are beginners in amassing a lot of money.

Again, we can't promise you a magic formula that will put one sizzling idea after another inside your head. What we can do, however, is give you our experience and some case histories that point up how you can develop your own creative ideas into good business ideas. A Power Shortcut helps at this point to focus your thinking.

Power Shortcut: Absolutely original ideas are few and far between. Instead of trying to dream up the truly novel idea, look at other people's successes and see what you can do to imitate them or improve on them.

This Power Shortcut is really an extension of one we gave you in Chapter 8 when we told you to copy someone else's success in the mail-order business. The concept is just as valid in any other business. If you can make something better, charge less, market it more efficiently, give it a little "twist" or something, then you're a long way forward in making a success. Now—how do you seek out profitable ideas to copy? Here are a few ways that immediatley come to our mind; you can probably add more if you spend some time thinking.

- Good business ideas are around you wherever you look. What about that restaurant that just opened in the same place that had a string of failures? What is different that the new owner is doing? Better food? Lower prices? Is he attracting a different "crowd" such as big-spending singles? Look at obviously successful businesses and try to answer questions like this. Look especially at businesses that have been turned around into successes.
- What about service in different businesses? Two gas stations compete side by side on the highway. One is always filled with cars while the other seems empty. Why? Does one owner jump up and wash windshields without being asked? Are the restrooms cleaner? Does he give stamps or premiums to encourage patronage?
- You see someone making it big in the real-estate business speculating and building in your town. What can you learn by looking? Was there a change in zoning laws that now permits garden apartments in a once residential zone? Are other changes contemplated? Is it worth spending 15 minutes with the town clerk and asking questions? You bet it is!

Getting rich by asking questions

Vernon K. is a person perhaps much like yourself. Each morning he rode to work on a bus and wondered about building a truly big income for himself. He passed through a town each day that was a very desirable suburb for people working in the nearby city. However, the town had been built up years ago and so no land was available for development. In addition, Vernon wasn't rich enough to speculate in a big way. These drawbacks didn't hold back his imagination one bit.

In a small notebook, Vernon jotted down facts and ideas

as he watched the passing scene through the bus window day after day. Then one day he started sorting out these very rough notes and this is what they looked like:

- Homes are very expensive in L----- (one of the towns he passed through).
- Homes are sold very quickly because the area is desirable.
- Parts of the town are old with ramshackle old houses, especially near the encroaching commercial district.
- Nobody wants these old houses because they would require too much investment to repair and maintain.
- With prices and taxes sky-high, there is a big demand for small homes—something not now available.
- Recently, certain parts of town were rezoned to permit building on smaller plots that might be available.

Of course, Vernon had other notes, but these are the important ones that leaped out at him and gave him the idea that eventually brought him close to a goal of making $100 an hour. As a little test of your own thinking power to come up with million-dollar ideas, what would you do given these facts?

Now compare your thinking with Vernon's. This is what he did:

1) He checked with the zoning office in L----- to see what parts of town had been rezoned to permit smaller building lots. In fact, he was given a map showing exactly what kind of building was permitted in each part of town.

2) On the weekend, Vernon drove around the town looking at the areas that had been rezoned. Most of these areas were filled with older homes—not very promising real-estate investments.

3) On one large lot in this part of town there stood a really run-down old house. Years and years ago it must have been a beautiful home standing on a piece of property about 100 by 200 feet.

4) Vernon checked the city records and discovered the house was owned by out-of-town heirs of the original owners. They couldn't care less about the place and were looking for someone to take it off their hands. But nobody wanted to buy the house after seeing what kind of money would be needed to make it livable again.

5) Because the owners had gotten so few nibbles on the property, they were willing for only $1000 to give Vernon an option to buy the property at a negotiated price within three months. This was all Vernon needed to get his money machine moving.

Vernon immediately discarded the idea of renovating the house, an idea that most people would come up with. Instead, he decided he would tear down the house and seek a subdivision of the property so he would come out with four 50-by-100 foot building lots, something now permitted by the new zoning law.

Four building lots, ready to build upon by some speculator, would bring almost as much as the negotiated price of the property. The next step was to contact some speculative builders in the area. Vernon told them he had these four building lots "sewed up" and would they be interested in a joint venture. He didn't have any trouble getting a reliable builder to say "yes" to his deal.

Vernon didn't realize it, but he was using an important Power Shortcut in setting up this deal

Power Shortcut: You don't have to own property in order to "sell" it. If you control it in some way, you can use it to make deals.

This may sound illegal, but it is a perfectly legitimate business device. In fact, it is used all the time in the stock and commodity markets when speculators buy "on margin." By having an option on the property no other builder could get the jump on Vernon and turn the old property to his own advantage. If a builder wanted part of the deal, he had to work with Vernon.

All Vernon had was the option, but working with a speculator, he was able to command a good part of the profits. Most of the profits had to go to the builder because he was the one who finally had to put up cash to build the houses. However, after the houses were built and sold, Vernon was $9000 richer. He estimated he spent a hundred or so hours running around, finding out facts, and handling details with the builder he picked. With that, his hourly "profit" came to $90—close to the goal of making $100 an hour.

We've dealt at length with Vernon's case history because we think it illustrates how boring hours spent looking out a bus window were transformed into $9000—the beginning of Vernon's climb to real wealth. Everyone, including yourself, has similar times in his life, and we hope this example inspires you to come up with your own $100-an-hour deal.

Simple ideas on the job can bring you a fortune

Regardless of the kind of job you now hold—whether it's in a factory, office, or in some service business that takes you traveling outside—you probably have the opportunity to come up with some idea related to your work that can make you money. All you have to do is to "fine tune" your creative ability. Here's how:

- Whenever you have a disagreeable job to do, stop complaining and try to think of a way to make the job easier, faster, or less costly. Is there some way you can profit from your idea, either with a patent, a copyright, or just by making some device that others will pay money for to do the same disagreeable job? A woman invented a disposable toilet-bowl mop using this technique.

- Try to think of products related to the one you're working on that can bring you a profit if sold to your boss, or exploited by yourself. We know a person who works for a publisher who came up with an idea for a newsletter—it was a perfectly obvious idea after it was explained—but the company was very willing to buy the idea outright for $50,000. No writing ability was needed, just the idea. For the time spent, this idea was worth $1000 an hour!

- How often have you been given instructions by your supervisor on how to do a particular job, and deep down you felt like saying, "Boy, is that a stupid way of doing it!" Well, try to come up with a better way. If the idea saves your boss money, *you* may be the next supervisor. Or you can take the idea to someone who will appreciate you even more.

- Always question any statement or procedure that is explained by saying "That's the way we've always done it!" In most cases, this is an excuse for laziness. Everything can be improved if you think about it long enough.

As a final piece of advice, we want to stress this important fact: an idea is absolutely worthless as long as it stays in your head. To make it pay off for you—perhaps to the extent of $100 an hour—you've got to put that idea into practice.

We've given you some cautions to observe, like not quitting your job too soon, and you can easily see other pitfalls. However, somewhere along the line you're going to have to make a big decision. We hope we've given you enough help in this chapter so you can make the decision that *makes you rich!*

11

using the power shortcuts to build an automatic income for life

What is an "automatic income"?

Don't look for a definition in any dictionary. The term automatic income is one we use to describe the kind of money you can make when you apply to the fullest the Power Shortcuts we've been describing. Specifically, an automatic income is one that:

- Puts money in your pocket day in and day out with very little work on your part;
- Gives you plenty of time to enjoy the good things of life—the big cars, the long vacations, the travel to parts of the world that others dream about;
- Sets you up "for life" with real security—money-making enterprises, and the respect of friends, associates, and important people in your community.

Actually, when you think about it for a moment or two, you will realize that our whole book has been showing you how to attain this goal. Through our Power Shortcuts and real-life case histories of people like yourself, we've tried to show that it is truly possible to make up to $100 an hour every hour you work and to turn that kind of money-making ability into an automatic income for life.

At this point it is important to review some concepts and to set you exactly on course to reach your big-money goal.

The Power Shortcuts

As used in this book, Power Shortcuts are valuable business hints and insights, many of which were learned painfully over a long period of time. They are a college education in starting, running, and building a small business into a $100-an-hour enterprise.

Don't think you can absorb them to the fullest in a single quick reading of this book. We urge you to keep referring to them now and in the future. Also, don't think that these are all the Power Shortcuts that exist. There are many more that others have discovered and used to build their fortunes.

However, the ones we've given you here are basic, and we feel they cover fully the essentials vital to your success. Give them every chance. You should also be alert to other Power Shortcuts that you will come across in your search for wealth.

You will find them out from your own experience and the experience of others, from speaking to successful people, and from reading other books such as this. Keep them in mind. Better yet, get a notebook and keep a permanent record of them.

Timing

When we say $100 an hour, that is precisely what we mean. Not $100 a day, not $100 a week, but *$100 an hour every hour you work!*

However, don't jump the gun at this point. In the beginning no one can promise you an immediate $100 an hour for a 40- to 60- hour week. That would be an instant $4000 to $6000 a week, or up to $300,000 a year. This is not to say that such an income should be beyond your dreams. Not by a long shot! You can do it with the help we've given you in these pages. It will take some patience on your part and some work.

In the beginning you should search for opportunities that can give you big money for relatively little investment of time, even if that time falls far short of a full work week. Recall the example of Vernon K. in Chapter 10 who put together a real-estate deal that netted him $9000 for about 100 hours of work. That came to $90 an hour, and you might be able to do a similar deal in somewhat less than 100 hours, and boost your hourly income to the magical level of $100 an hour. However, it is unlikely that you can put together such deals, back to back, 40 hours a week for a prolonged length of time right from the start.

But this is the important thing to remember: Each time you make some deal, you will find that making big money becomes easier and easier to achieve. Like many other activities, you can improve your skill and get into the habit of making money!

Building up to $100 an hour

The secret of making $100 an hour, or $800 a day, or even $4000 a week, is to build up to that figure by several routes. Within these pages, we've given you dozens of stories and examples of ways others have made money and how you can adapt their techniques to your own profit. We want to emphasize the point we made over and over again: Try a lot of things to find the one or more things that work best for you.

If you find an opportunity that earns you a modest amount of money, don't discard the idea immediately. It may be possible to bring in helpers or assistants to do the actual work and pay you a profit that really is quite substantial when figured out on an hourly basis. For example:

Let's say you start a typing service like Carrie W. did in Chapter 4. Carrie got typing assignments at the local university and farmed them out to a crew of typists she had gathered together. She paid her typists only when they worked, and Carrie's profit was the difference between what she paid her typists and what she charged the users of her service. This difference was quite small: Carrie earned about $1 an hour for each hour that a typist worked for her. But look at how the arithmetic added up to make Carrie's real income $40 an hour in a typical instance:

- 4 typists each worked 10 hours for a total of 40 hours
- 40 hours of typing work produced $40 profit for Carrie
- Carrie spent one hour at the university picking up the assignments and distributing them to her staff of free-lance typists.
- Hourly income for Carrie: $40 an hour.

This example should make abundantly clear to you the magic of up-scaling small enterprises. In a nutshell, you can build a huge mountain from a lot of small stones.

Our final word to you is not to be discouraged from early failures. All of us have to go through some disappointments. We trust that we have minimized that possibility to the limit with the advice we have been able to give you.

We would also like to hear about your successes. While it is not possible to answer all the letters we receive because of the volume of mail, it is entirely possible that your name and experience could appear in a future book. Just write to us in care of the publisher of this book whose address appears on the title page and tell us your particular success story.

Good luck!

index

A

Abilities, 32
Activities:
    different, 74
    testing, 48
Ads, 40
Advertising:
    free, 68, 192-194
    operating necessity, 53
    radio, 187
    space, 187
    television, 187
    word-of-mouth, 79
Advice, free, 94-96
Age, 27
Ambition, 31, 53
Assignments, outsize, 42
Assistance, 133-134
Attitude, positive, 76
Attorneys, 114, 137
Automatic income, 210-213
Ayer's Guide, 95, 161

B

Baby-sitting in home, 133
Bank:
    industrial, 109
    mutual savings, 108-109

Barriers:
    ask for help, 73
    be aware of risks, 70-71
    direct attack, 68, 69-73
    don't give up easily, 69-70
    exploring new things, 73
    image of success, 76-78
    indirect attack, 68
    joining the experts, 78-80
    keep goals in mind, 73
    make success a habit, 80-81
    making every minute count, 73
    new ideas, 71
    people leverage, 118-121
    potential within you, 73-75
    smashing, 65-81
    thinking quickly, 71-72
    work with people, 69
Biographies, 80
Bird baths, 149
Bird feeders, 149
Birdhouse kits, 146-150
Bookstore, 91
Boss, being, 42
Broker, 139
Bulk mail permits, 181
Business certificate application, 138
Business consultant, 114
Businesses for Sale, 87
Business magazines, 95, 96
Business Opportunities column, 40
Business reply mail, 181-182

C

Capital:
   expansion, 121
   lack, 66
   raising, 61-62
Carpet-cleaning, 30
Cash, never lay out, 86
Cash flow, 169
Catalog, 149
Charities, 106
Charts:
   rate, 21-25
   self-evaluation, 43
Checklist:
   frame of mind, 35-37
   goals, 26
   job-elimination, 124-127
Cheshire labels or tapes, 175
Circular handling, 174-175
Cleaning business, 122
"Close-out" kits, 149
Clubs, investment, 108
Collection problems, 100
Colleges, 105-106
Color-photo lab, 75
Color processing, 49
Commissions, state development, 106
Companies, money sources, 109
Company name, recording, 137
Competitors, 142
Consultants:
   business, 114
   handyman, 134
   investment, 109
   need no space, 139
   staff, 139
Consumable parts, 171
Contracts, 85-86
Cooking, 40-42
Co-op mailings, 188
Coordinating services, 139-140
Copy, 185
Corporation, 137
Costs, 175-176
Courses, 67, 136, 154-156
Credit reputation, 110

D

Debt, 109
Delegation of responsibility, 117
Delivery service broker, 139
Development commissions, 106
Directory, 67-68, 190

Diversification, 78, 91
Doctors, 114
Doers, 20
Do-it-yourself craze, 133-134
Drains, cleaning, 29-30, 79
Dry-cleaning store, 38-40

E

Embossing machine, 50
Employees, 30, 60-61, 77, 84, 85, 93, 197
Employment agencies, 87
Envelopes:
   color, 184
   extraordinary, 183
   first impression, 182
   glassine window, 184
   message, 184-185
   size, 183
Expansion:
   capital, 121
   people leverage, 117
   planning, 59, 93
Experiences, new, 37-38, 48, 73, 74
Experts, 78-80
Extension mailings, 167, 168

F

Facilities:
   meanings of word, 103
   selling, 140
Factors, 108
Fast-food restaurant franchise, 42
Financing, 53
Finder, 108
Foundations, 106
Fountains, 149
Friends, 107
Funds, pension, 107-108

G

Garage sales, 130
Garden items, 149
Gillette, 171
Goals:
   business magazines, 95, 96
   checklist, 26
   figure possible losses, 89
   formula to attain, 83
   free professional advice, 94-96
   hiring moonlighters, 86-87
   home operation, 86
   how to reach, 26-27

Goals *(cont.)*
   jobs simple, 89
   keep in mind, 73
   long-term investments, 90-91
   low labor costs, 89
   mailing lists, 88
   middle income markets, 88
   need for business, 83
   never lay out cash, 86
   order before work, 85-86
   people leverage, 93
   personal involvement, 90
   plan for expansion, 93
   planning and setting, 82
   profit potential, 88-90
   pyramid, 92-94
   serve small segment of market, 91-92
   setting, 21
   specializing, 91-92
   trade magazines, 94-96
   what not to do, 87-88

H

Habit, success, 54, 80-81
Helpers, 29-30, 60-61, 77, 84, 85, 93, 197
Home business:
   assistance, 133-134
      baby-sitting, 133
      consultant, 134
      do-it-yourself craze, 133-134
      help plan building project, 133
      "staff of consultants," 134
   broker, 139
   business certificate application, 138
   competitors doing poor job, 142
   consultant, 139
   coordinating services, 139-140
   corporation, 137
   few competitors, 142
   finding right one, 141-143
   future sales, 135
   importing, 138
   legal and financial protection, 137
   make time of others count, 140
   manufacturing, 131-133
      easy to make product
      high mark-up, 132
      meaning, 131
      minimum of skill, 132
      no expensive materials, 132
      no large competition, 132
      produce it easily, 132
      simple equipment, 132
   no investment, 140-141

Home business *(cont.)*
   no space needed, 139-140
   offer better service, 142
   people already customers, 136
   record company name, 137
   research, 134-136
   self facilities of others, 140
   selling, 129-131
      door to door, 131
      garage sales, 130
      illustration, 131
      mail-order, 130 (*see also* Mail-order selling)
      manufacturer's representative, 130
      many different ways, 130
      many types of products, 130
      telephone, 131
      to businesses, 131
      very practical, 130
   selling products you don't own, 138
   serve many at a time, 137
   SMART, 129-137
   telephone, 137, 138
   training, 136-137
      courses, 136
      selling supplies, 136-137
Home improvement loans, 110
Home operation, 86
Home-security business, 77
Hours, 33
How to Borrow Everything You Need to Build a Great Personal Fortune, 80
"How-to-do-it" books, 91

I

Ideas, 204, 208-209
Idea-starters, 53
Image, 76-78
Importing, 138
Impulsiveness, 71
Income supplementing activity, 53
Individual, needs and ambitions, 53
Individual investors, 107
Industrial banks, 109
Insurance, 103-104
Insurance companies, 108
Intentions, 25
Interests, 32
Investment clubs, 108
Investment companies, small business, 107
Investment consultants, 109

Investment groups, private, 106
Investments:
    long-term, 90-91
    none needed, 140-141
    time, not money, 101
Investors, individual, 107
Involvement, personal, 90
"I" thinking, 119

J

Job, 195-209
Job-elimination checklist, 124-127

K

Kits:
    birdhouse, 146-148
    "close-out," 149
    "sale," 149

L

Labor costs, 89
Lawyers, 114, 137
Leasing companies, 109
Lenders, 101-112 (*see also* Other people's money)
Letters, business, 59
Leverage:
    people, 113-127
    word, 51-52
Lily pools, 149
List broker, 149, 156, 168
List rental, 175
List rental income, 149, 156
Loans, sources, 121
Long-term investments, 90-91
Losses, figuring ahead, 89
Luck, 25, 48-50

M

Magic Money Pyramid, 39
Mailing lists:
    competitors, 88
    renting, 159-160
    successful, 162-166
    testing, 177-179
Mail-order selling:
    additions to product line, 150
    advantages, 144
    ask for order directly, 158, 159
    birdhouse kits, 146-150
    brochure, 152
    cash flow, 169
    catalog, 149

Mail-order selling *(cont.)*
    caution, 167
    choosing right lists, 152
    classified ads, 147
    "close-out" kits, 149
    consumable parts, 171
    courses, 67, 154-156
    customers all over world, 144
    extension mailings, 167, 168
    Gillette razor, 171
    growth capital, 144
    list broker, 149, 156, 168
    list rental income, 149, 156
    magazines appealing to interest groups, 159
    market research, 150-152
    mimeographed reply letter, 147
    money-back guarantee, 157
    moonlighters, 149
    more income from each customer, 171
    names rented, 149
    nature and garden items, 149
    100-postcard trick, 150-152
    picking mailing list, 162-166
        discover "hot" ones, 165-166
        rating, 163-165
        source and age of names, 163
    pitfall, 145-146
    popular products and services, 152
    potential customers, 157
    pre-packaged plan, 145-146
    pricing product, 152
    publication in which to advertise, 160-162
    pyramiding, 144, 148, 167-169
    records, 148
    related items of interest, 149, 170
    renting mailing lists, 159-160
    repeat income, 169-171
    "sale" kits, 149
    seasonal line of items, 171
    send for more information, 158, 159
    specialized newsletters, 154-156
        current events, 154
        digest and reprint news, 154
    start on shoestring, 144
    "success secret" techniques, 173-194
        (*see also* "Success secret" Techniques)
    test ideas on small scale, 148, 156
    time of year, 168-169
    what others do in business, 147
    what product or services, 152-153
        alternate sources of supply, 152
        at least 66% discount off list, 153

index

Mail-order selling *(cont.)*
    books, other publications, 153-154
    interesting or satisfying, 152
    inventory, 153
    items seldom in stores, 153, 157
    order you can't fill, 152
    packing and shipping, 153
    realistic prices, 152, 153, 157
    work at any hour, 144
Management chores, 53
Manufacturer's representative, 130
Manufacturing, 131-133
Markets, 121
Master Rate Charts, 21-25
Matchbooks, 187-188
Mental attitude, positive, 76
Middle-income bracket, 88
Mini-trips, 37
Money:
  ask for more than you need, 111
  get all you need, 61-62
  Other People's Money, 97-112 *(see also* Other People's Money)
  reason you want, 102
  sources, 105-109 *(see also* Other people's money)
  uses, 111
Moonlighters, 86-87, 149
Mortgage money, 110
Motor-repair, 154-156
Mower repair, 67
Multiplier effect, 121
Mutual savings banks, 108-109

N

Nature items, 149
Need for business, 83
Needs, individual, 53
New customers, finding, 116, 117, 121
Newsletter, 99, 154-156
Newspapers, 40
New things, experiencing, 37-38, 48, 73, 74

O

Offer, 102-103
100-postcard trick, 150-152
Operating, 53
Orders:
  as good as cash, 99
  before work, 85-86
  repeat, 101
Other People's Money:
  getting, 101-112
    ask for more than you need, 111
    charities and foundations, 106

Other People's Money *(cont.)*
    colleges and schools, 105-106
    credit reputation, 110
    facilities, 103
    factors, 108
    finder, 108
    individual investors, 107
    industrial banks, 109
    instant cash, 104-105
    insurance, 103-104
    insurance companies, 108
    investment clubs, 108
    investment consultants, 109
    leasing companies, 109
    mutual savings banks, 108-109
    offer, 102-103
    other companies, 109
    pension funds, 107-108
    personal qualities, 102
    private investment groups, 106
  getting:
    P.R.O.F.I.T. System, 102-104
    prospectus, 104
    Ready Reserve, 104-105
    reason you want money, 102
    relatives and friends, 107
    savings and loan associations, 107
    small business administration, 107
    small business investment companies, 107
    sources, 105-109
    state development commissions, 106
    time, 104
    Veterans Administration, 108
    when you are in debt, 109-112
    your suppliers, 106
  home improvement loans, 110
  invest time, not money, 101
  make it work for you, 98-101
  more profitable uses, 111
  mortgage money, 110
  newsletter, 99
  sell to businesses, 98-101
    "business related" products, 98
    costs less, 100
    fewer collection problems, 100
    personally usable products, 98
    promises to buy, 99-101
    repeat businesses, 101

P

Painting contractor, 84-90
Part-time businesses, 195-209 *(see also* Time)

Pensions, 31, 32
Pension funds, 107-108
People leverage:
   barriers you erect, 118-121
      can do it better, 118, 119, 120-121
      can't afford outside help, 118, 119-120
      can't find right people, 118, 119, 120
   business consultant, 114
   delegating responsibility, 117
   developing new product lines, 121
   doctors, 114
   expansion, 93
   free yourself for big jobs, 118
   full-time on important decisions, 117, 118
   getting new customers, 116, 117, 121
   high P/L jobs, 126-127
   how you are progressing, 123-124
   increase your power, 114
   incredible results, 122
   individual efforts of many, 122
   "I" thinking, 119
   job-elimination checklist, 124-127
   lawyer, 114
   less time on small jobs, 117
   loans and capital, 121
   low P/L jobs, 125
   medium P/L jobs, 125-126
   multiplier effect, 121-122
   multiply chances for success, 114
   open up opportunities, 114
   others do what you want, 60
   perfectionist, 115
   personal involvement, 90
   pinpoint wasted hours, 124
   pyramids, 121
   searching out new markets, 121
   self-discovery, 118
   trial and error, 115
Perfectionists, 115
Personal involvement, 90
Personality:
   admit your faults, 63
   associate with successful people, 63
   avoid talking about yourself, 63
   believe others like you, 63-64
   build self-esteem of associates, 63
   interested in others, 63
   positive, 62-63
   winning, 62-64
Personal qualities, 102
Photo-equipment, 50
Photography, 75

Place to work, 58-59
Plumbing drain lines, 79
Positive Mental Attitude, 76
Postage, 175, 182
Post office, 179-182
Potential, 65, 73-75, 88
Printer, 191
Printing, 174
Private investment groups, 106
Problems, individual, 54
Product lines, 121
Products:
"business related," 98
   development and expansion, 59
   mail-order, 152-153
   personally usable, 98
Professional advice, free, 94-96
Profit potential, 88
P.R.O.F.I.T. system:
   facilities, 103
   insurance, 103-104
   offer, 102-103
   personal qualities, 102
   reason you want money, 102
   time, 104
Progress, 26, 57, 58
Projects, different, 47
Property, 207-208
Prospectus, 104
Publications, 59
Publishing journals, 91
Purchasing agents, 131
Purpose, intense, 48
Pyramiding, 92-94, 144, 148, 167-169
Pyramids in Egypt, 121

Q

Qualities, personal, 102
Questions, 205

R

Radio advertising, 187
Radio repairs, 43-44
Rate Charts, 21-25
Razor, 171
Ready Reserve, 104-105
Real estate broker, 139
Reason you want money, 102
Records, time and progress, 57-58
Referrals, 79
Related items of interest, 149, 170
Relatives, 107
Repeat sales, 101, 150, 169-171
Research, 134-136

index

Reserve money, 104-105
Responsibility, delegation ,117
Restaurants, 40-42
Retirement, 31, 32
Rewards, 26
Risks, 46-47, 53, 70-71

S

"Sale" kits, 149
Savings and loan associations, 107
Schedule, 58
Schools, 105-106
Seasonal line of items, 171
Security, home, 77
Self-discovery, process, 118
Self-evaluation chart, 43
"Self-help" books, 91
Selling, 53, 129-131
Serendipity, 49-50, 77
Services, 53, 152-153
Sewer cleaning, 79
Singlemindedness, 48
Skills:
   list, 43
   polish up, 74
   use ones you have, 31, 32
Small business administration, 107
Small business investment companies, 107
Sources of money, 105-109
Space, 139-140
Space advertising, 187
Specializing, 91-92
Stamps, 182
Standard Rate and Data Service, 95, 161, 192
State development commissions, 106
Stationery, 137, 138
Stories of success, 80-81
"Success secret" Techniques:
   analyzing project, 174
   business reply mail, 181-182
   co-op mailings, 188
   direct mail checklist, 174-176
      add costs carefully, 175-176
      circular handling, 174-175
      list rental, 175
      postage, 175
      printing, 174
   envelopes, 182-185
      color, 184
      extraordinary, 183
      glassine window, 184
      message, 184-185
      size, 183

"Success secret" Techniques *(cont.)*
   first impressions, 182
   four-part formula, 185-187
      Hey!, 185-186
      See?, 186
      So!, 186-187
      You!, 186
   free advertising, 192-194
   how many lists to test, 177-178
   how much you should expect, 176-177
   local post office, 180-182
   matchbooks, 187-188
   number of names to test, 178-179
   postage stamps, 182
   printer, 191-192
   radio and television advertising, 187
   space advertising, 187
   success on shoestring, 188-191
   test mailing, 177
   write copy that sells, 185
Sundials, 149
Suppliers, 106
Supplies, selling, 136-137

T

Talents, 25
Talkers, 20
Techniques, understanding and use, 32
Telephone, 131, 137, 138
Television advertising, 187
Test mailing, 177
Thinking:
   checklist, 35-37
   feel good about yourself, 35
   quickly, 71-72
Time:
   checklist of wealth hours, 201-202
      early morning, 201
      enforced period of idleness, 202
      evening, 201-202
      going to work, 201
      lunchtime, 201
      returning home, 201
      vacations, 202
      waiting for supper, 201
      weekends, 202
   cut amount needed, 54
   make every minute count, 73
   make time of others count, 140
   making the most, 56-57
   measuring value, 57-58
   people leverage, 117, 118
   plan, 202-204
   productive use, 55

Time *(cont.)*
    P.R.O.F.I.T. system, 104
    record, 57, 58
    rigid work schedule, 58
    sacrifice, 55
    wasted, 200
Timing, 211-212
Trade magazine, 94, 95, 96
Training, 136-137
Trips, 37-38
Typing service, 93-94

V

Veterans Administration, 108

W

"Wealth Plan," 28
Working for someone else, 195-209 *(see also* Time)